"Dr. David Clarke knows people. Dr. David Clarke knows humor. Dr. David Clarke knows his Bible. These come together in the perfect storm to put passion back in your marriage."

Dr. Woodrow Kroll, president of
Back to the Bible International

"If you've lost that loving feeling but would like to get it back again—and in the process take your marriage to a whole new level—then *Kiss Me Like You Mean It* is a book you'll have a hard time putting down. It is humorous, witty, well-written, but most of all practical! David's keen insights from the Song of Solomon will help you see marriage from a new perspective and free you to enjoy the deep levels of passion and intimacy that God designed us to enjoy in a healthy marriage relationship."

Gary J. Oliver, Ph.D., executive director of The Center for
Relationship Enrichment at John Brown University
and author of *Mad About Us: Moving from
Anger to Intimacy with Your Spouse*

"Dr. Clarke's book is a clarion call to the reality that marriage is not a business relationship but a warm, intimate interface of two unique individuals becoming one, and that this relationship can be kept vibrant and meaningful by a romance that need never grow cold. It will help reignite the fire that has grown cold for many."

Harold J. Sala, Ph.D., founder and president
of Guidelines International

KISS ME
Like You Mean It

Solomon's *Crazy in Love* How-To Manual

Dr. David Clarke

Revell
a division of Baker Publishing Group
Grand Rapids, Michigan

Published by Revell
a division of Baker Publishing Group
P.O. Box 6287, Grand Rapids, MI 49516-6287
www.revellbooks.com

Printed in the United States of America

Library of Congress Cataloging-in-Publication Data
Clarke, David, Dr.
    Kiss me like you mean it : Solomon's crazy in love how-to manual / David Clarke.
        p.   cm.
    ISBN 978-0-8007-3329-2 (pbk.)
    1. Bible. O.T. Song of Solomon—Criticism, interpretation, etc. I. Title.
BS1485.52.C53 2009
223'.906—dc22   2008047710

Scripture is taken from the New American Standard Bible®, Copyright © 1960, 1962, 1963, 1968, 1971, 1972, 1973, 1975, 1977, 1995 by The Lockman Foundation. Used by permission.

To Bill and Kathy Clarke,
who have had a Song of Solomon love
for over fifty years

Contents ·

Contents

1

"Help! I'm Living with an Alien!"

Why doesn't passion between a man and a woman last? Why, in 100 percent of all marriages, does passion disappear just a handful of years after the wedding? What kills that glorious, heart-pumping, electric, sexually charged feeling of love and desire?

I have the answer. And it's not pretty.

After two decades of intense marital research, I have discovered the shocking truth about passion. To cushion the emotional blow you're about to receive, I urge you to sit down, take a deep breath, and hug your favorite stuffed animal to your chest. Ready? Here are my findings.

Something completely unexpected and terrible happens two to fourteen years into a marriage. The person you fell passionately in love with is replaced by an alien. I'm not kidding. The alien looks exactly like the wonderful person you married, but its behavior is bizarre, unbelievably annoying, and obviously designed to drive you insane.

You and your spouse used to have so much in common. You enjoyed the same activities. You laughed at the same things. Your feelings and thoughts were so in tune. You were soul mates. But now you and this alien have virtually nothing in common. The differences between you could fill a book. Actually, an entire library.

My research has also revealed that aliens always replace *both spouses* in a marriage. In my twenty-one years as a clinical psychologist, I've worked with a lot of married couples. Hundreds and hundreds. Marital therapy is my specialty. Every husband and wife has said words like these to me privately: "Doc, who is this person I'm now living with? You wouldn't believe the changes I've seen in my spouse. I want the person I married to come back!"

I'm telling you, it's aliens. Here are some alien transformation stories. Draw your own conclusions.

Communication

When the man was dating you, ladies, he could communicate. He actually talked to you and shared personal things. Now, his communication skills have vanished. He has very little to say to you. Everything in his life is a secret. It's as if he's joined the CIA and all of his information—thoughts, feelings, opinions—is on a "need to know" basis. And, apparently, he believes you don't need to know much at all.

Almost every day you ask him, "What happened today?" He almost always responds with the one word that drives you crazy: "Nothing." You'd like to reply, "Nothing? Really?

Were you drugged when you got to work and tossed into a storeroom for the entire day?"

He's angry, agitated, and irritable. Obviously, something is bothering him. You ask a simple question motivated by compassion: "Honey, what's wrong?" He slams the door, conversationally speaking, on your fingers with his trusty one-word answer: "Nothing." Now *you're* angry, agitated, and irritable. You know good and well something's wrong! How can you help, if he won't tell you? How can you get to know him better and build intimacy, if he won't tell you?

The man's other tried-and-true response is: "I don't know."

Woman: "How was your day?"

Man: "I don't know."

Woman: "What did you think of the movie?"

Man: "I don't know."

Woman: "When do you want to discuss finances?"

Man: "I don't know."

Woman: "How do you feel about what I just said about our marriage?"

Man: "I don't know."

With these three words, he indicates there may be some information in his head, but he is unable to access it at this time. He'd love to talk, but unfortunately, he's drawing a blank. Of course, you're on to him and his little game. No one draws a blank that often. Either he's in the early stages of dementia, or he just doesn't want to talk to you.

When you were dating the woman, husband, you knew she was expressive. She'd talk about all kinds of things, and you enjoyed listening to her. You didn't mind. Now you mind, because it seems as though she talks five times as much. She's gone from being a medium-size waterfall to Niagara Falls. She is drowning you in her torrent of words!

She wants you to know absolutely everything that happens to her every day. No event is too small to share. And you will hear not only what happened, though she'll cover that in incredible, minute detail. You'll also have to hear her feelings, her thoughts, the feelings and thoughts of the other persons who were there, the feelings and thoughts of persons who weren't there but to whom she talked and found out their feelings and thoughts, past events in her life that this current event triggered, and what the event means about her, you, and your relationship.

If you can somehow gut your way through her detail-studded monologue, you're not done yet. She's not just telling a story. She wants your feedback, and she's going to ask you for it. Repeatedly. She'll pepper you with all kinds of questions. She wants to know your thoughts, responses, reactions, and feelings. It's like living with a private investigator who's always probing for information. She wants to know how her experience of this event impacts you and resonates with you and your relationship with her. She wants to know how this event has helped you to understand her better. All you can think to say is:

"I wasn't even there!"

"I don't know."

"Nothing occurs to me."

"Who cares?"

"I'm not interested in the lives and problems of the four women you were in line with at the grocery store while you waited for a price check on lima beans."

"Can you wrap this up? I'm hungry."

None of these reactions will please her, and you'll be in trouble. Unfortunately, it's not over yet. Now, you'll have to hear—in detail and with intensity—how upset and hurt she is with your pathetic and uncaring responses to an important event in her life.

Memory

He has the memory of an amoeba. He forgets nearly everything, except all the vital statistics of his favorite sports teams. He can't remember the items you asked him to get at the store. He can't remember the chore he agreed to do. He can't remember the party on Friday, the one you've been telling him about for a month. He can't remember so many things you know you've told him—to his face.

When you remind him of something he's forgotten, he replies with the same two, lame lines: "I forgot," and, "You never told me that!" In the areas of his personal life, your relationship, and communications between the two of you, he can recall only the last half hour of his life. And, that's on a good day. So, when he says, "I don't know," there's a pretty good chance he's telling the truth.

She has the memory of an elephant. She hardly ever forgets anything. She has an uncanny ability to recreate scenes and conversations that occurred decades ago. "Bob, a discussion about my mother took place in our kitchen twelve years ago. It was a Wednesday evening, seven o'clock. I was sitting at the table, and you were slouching against the counter. I was wearing a blue top and white slacks. You had on a chili-stained T-shirt and those old, ratty, red gym shorts. I began the discussion by saying I didn't appreciate your comment about Mother's cooking. . . ."

Level of Sensitivity

The man you dated and fell in love with was understanding, sensitive, and mature. You were certain you'd landed the next Prince Charming. Now, you're beginning to realize you ended up with Goofy. His behavior is often crude, offensive, and adolescent. You'd call him an animal, but you don't want to insult animals.

When you eat at a restaurant, he rips off the end of the paper covering his straw and blows the paper tube into the air. The fancier the restaurant, the better he likes it. You never know where the straw paper will go (into someone's drink, someone's hair, down someone's shirt), and that's part of the fun. He likes to read in the bathroom. He calls it "the reading room" or "the library" and can spend up to twenty minutes in there. It's the only time he can multitask. Of course, a well-timed belch or passing of gas is always good for a laugh.

Husband, your wife is increasingly disgusted with your behavior. You believe you're perfectly normal and that her standards are too high. You didn't realize you married royalty. She prides herself on being a refined and elegant person with excellent tastes, who values socially appropriate behavior. She used to find your antics funny and endearing. Now, she looks down her nose at you. It's no fun being married to Miss Manners.

Entertainment Choices

Before you married her, and for the first few years of your marriage, the two of you seemed to enjoy the same television shows and movies. You'd watch together, and it was a lot of fun. Now, she will watch only serious dramas and romantic comedies. She loves a lot of talking, a lot of crying, a main character taking forever to die, and long, drawn-out romances.

You watched *A Walk to Remember* with her. It's the tragic story of a teenage girl who is slowly dying of leukemia. She and her boyfriend get closer and closer as she fades away. Talk about depressing. But the longest death scene ever filmed is the horribly burned man in *The English Patient*. This extremely disfigured guy talks about his ill-fated romance with some chick for three solid hours! Every man who is forced to watch this nightmare of a movie thinks the same thing: "I can't take this much longer. I'm going to die before he does. Would someone please suffocate him with a pillow and put him—and me—out of our misery?"

But the ultimate chick movie is *Pride and Prejudice*, Jane Austen's classic story of the Victorian romance of Mr. Darcy and Elizabeth Bennet, one of five sisters seeking suitable husbands. I'm not talking about the two-hour version. Oh, no. I refer to the gold standard of the *Pride and Prejudice* films: the six-hour marathon miniseries produced by the BBC and the A&E Network.

This six-hour drama documents—in excruciating detail—the longest romance in the history of the world. For the unfortunate man viewing this sort of, kind of, maybe-but-not-quite, it'll-take-a-little-longer romance, the experience rivals childbirth in terms of pain and suffering. Finally, at the end of six of the longest hours of your life, Mr. Darcy and Miss Bennet get together. There's a lot of sitting around and talking, a tremendous amount of whimpering and sobbing, and not one person dies!

Why couldn't Mr. Darcy, in the first half hour of the movie, simply walk up to Elizabeth and say, "Hey, I like you. Do you want to go out on a date? And, by the way, I'm filthy rich." I'll tell you why. Because that would defeat the purpose of a chick flick, which is to entertain women and torture men.

At the end of every chick flick you endure, your wife will be crying. You'll be crying too, but for different reasons. You're upset because you've wasted precious hours of your life watching this piece of sappy drivel, and now you'll have to listen to her drone on and on about the movie and what it means about her, about every woman she's ever known, and about your relationship.

You really thought your man liked your type of entertainment. Why, he watched dramas and romantic comedies with you and seemed to enjoy them! You were sure he was different from all the other guys. But that was before marriage. Before the alien showed up. Later in the marriage, it dawned on you that he had been humoring you so you'd marry him.

You can handle the sports he watches. That's not too bad. But how is it possible that one of his favorite actors is Jim Carrey? He'll watch both *Ace Ventura* movies and *The Mask* over and over! His all-time favorite comedy is *Dumb and Dumber*. He laughs until he's sick at the same old nasty, offensive parts. You're forced to face the fact that you're married to a man with an emotional age of twelve.

If it isn't gross-out, insipid comedies, it's brutally violent action movies. When the body count doesn't top fifty, he's seriously disappointed. Death and gore and destruction and absolutely no plot are what he looks for in an action-adventure movie. And Mr. Cro-Magnon Man wants you to watch this kind of movie with him! You're beginning to think that you should have had him take an I.Q. test before marrying him.

Sex

You were both absolutely certain that sex would not be a problem in your marriage. You were very attracted to each other and your physical relationship during courtship was exciting, beautiful, and natural. But as with every other area of your relationship, after the wedding tremendous differences surfaced in your lovemaking.

The woman remembers *everything* . . . except the last time she had sex with her husband. The man remembers *nothing* . . . except the last time he had sex with his wife. One spouse— usually the husband, but not always—desires sex a lot more than the other spouse.

The woman needs to be prepared for sex with communication, teamwork with the chores and kids, and romance. The man needs only an erection to be prepared for sex. The problem is, he thinks his erection is all the woman needs to be ready too.

The woman likes to be approached for sex in a subtle, gentle, and loving way. The man's idea of a subtle, gentle, and loving way is to pinch her bottom and say, "Let's do it."

The woman prefers—needs—a slow, careful, and gradual progression in foreplay and intercourse. The man prefers speed. He's proud that he can complete foreplay and intercourse in five minutes or fewer. He may get his name in the Guinness Book of World Records, but it will become extremely unsatisfying and frustrating for his wife.

Goodbye, Passion

The bad news is, I've only touched on a few of the differences that disrupt your relationship after marriage. I could easily fill a six-volume set with the avalanche of differences that rush into your once passionate marriage. Your spouse doesn't get replaced by an alien, but it surely seems that way.

All these differences crush your passion. You don't know how to make the adjustments and so you do your best to find ways to survive and cope. Add children, the stress of finances and careers, and the speed and chaos of everyday life, and you have zero chance to keep the flame of passion burning.

Oh, you're still married and that's good. You still love each other and that's good. But you're not having much fun, are you? You're not madly in love, are you? There's a world of difference between being in love and being *passionately in love*.

Welcome to the Club

Well, join the "No More Passion Club." It's a big one. A very big one. Believe me, you're not alone. The loss of passion in marriage is universal. Sooner or later, it happens to every married couple. It might be two years, seven years, ten years, or fourteen years after the wedding. But the loss of passion will get you.

It got my wife Sandy and me. We had been married for about ten years. In those ten years we had three baby girls. Our little darlings were taking a major bite out of our passion. Emily, Leeann, and Nancy were consuming our lives. They spent all their time—and all our time—screaming, crying, whining, belching, spitting up, pooping, making massive messes in every room in the house, demanding attention, creating huge loads of laundry, and eating all the food in sight.

Life was unbelievably busy. Life was stressful. Life was numbingly monotonous. Life was all about the kids, my career, friends, making enough money to pay the bills and put food on the table, and church. Life was all about everything and everybody but Sandy and me.

Sound familiar? I'll bet it does. The loss of passion happens so gradually you're not even aware of it. Until one day you suddenly see with sickening clarity that it's gone. Typically, one spouse realizes the passion is gone before the other.

It dawned on me one day that something important, something precious, was missing from our love relationship. That something was passion. I went to Sandy and told her. She agreed.

Over the next few months, as Sandy and I discussed the state of our marriage, we decided passion was something we couldn't live without. We didn't want to be just parents. Roommates. Good friends. That's not why we got married! We got married because we were passionately in love with each other. Period. And we were determined to get that passionate feeling back and keep it.

How about Your Passion?

Be honest. Your infatuation has fizzled out. Your many differences are painfully apparent. Annoying habits have set in. One child (or more) is in your home. And that child is not leaving home for a long time. Or, maybe it's just the two of you in your home, and you've realized there is no spark left in your marriage. The routines of life have taken over. Your passion is dead. Or, at least, it's in bad shape. Your relationship is blah. Ho-hum. Boring.

You wonder: "Can we ever get our passion back? Can we ever again be crazy in love?" God has an answer for you. It is a big yes! You can't help losing your passion. That happens to every married couple. What you can do is what Sandy and I did. You can get it back.

There is a book, from God himself, the most beautiful and powerful love story ever told. It was given to you to show you how to get the passion back into your relationship and how to keep it there until life ends.

The book is the Song of Solomon. It is a magnificent, sublime poem describing the godly, passionate love between Solomon and his wife. I have chosen to use the name "Shulamith" for Solomon's wife. For reasons known only to Solomon (and God, of course), he does not give her a specific, formal name. But I believe, as do several other commentators on the Song, that Solomon likely used "Shulamith" as a personal pet name for his beloved. She was a real person of great physical and emotional beauty, and I think she deserves a beautiful and personal name: Shulamith.

Of the over one thousand such songs Solomon wrote, God has saved this special book for us. God wants every couple to be as crazy in love as Solomon and Shulamith. And, God wants you to stay that way throughout your marriage. Loving with passion is God's design for marriage. To live without passion is not healthy—in fact, it's downright destructive.

In the Song of Solomon, God provides a "Crazy in Love How-To Manual." The Song is a detailed explanation of how a husband and a wife can experience unending passion, and have a blast doing it! This amazing book of the Bible teaches you how to break through your many differences and relationship obstacles to a powerful, permanent passion.

The Path to Passion

In chapter two, I cover the myths about passion and about the Song of Solomon. A lot of experts are dead wrong about marital passion. A lot of other experts are wrong about the teaching of the Song. Someone has to set the record straight, and I'm that guy.

In chapters three through twenty, I teach the *passion principles* contained in the Song of Solomon. There are two chapters for each principle: one chapter describes the mistakes couples make, followed by a second chapter that explains—with teaching from the Song—how couples can master that passion principle. I devote three chapters to resolving conflict and preparing for physical intimacy. Finally, in chapter twenty-one, I examine Song of Solomon 8:6–7, the beautiful definition of Solomon and Shulamith's love.

Ready to get your passion back? Let's go.

2 ·

Can Passion Really Last, and What Does Solomon Know about It Anyway?

From the time Solomon wrote his beautiful song of love some 3,000 years ago, there have been myths about the book itself and about passion in marriage. These myths—both secular and Judeo-Christian—have confused lovers for centuries and done great damage to many couples. It's time to explode these myths and replace them with God's truth about marital passion.

Myth #1: Passion Can't Last in a Marriage, So Find a New Spouse (Secular, Popular Culture)

Look, passion never lasts in a marriage. Never. It's just the nature of the beast. Your male-female differences catch up to you. Life becomes routine. You begin to bore each other. The only excitement comes from your ever-increasing conflicts. If you have kids, they drive the last few nails into the coffin of your passion. Some couples keep their passion longer than others, but no couple ever keeps it forever. If you get seven, ten, fifteen, or even twenty years of passion with your spouse, consider yourself very lucky. When passion leaves, it's gone. It isn't ever coming back with your current spouse.

When you realize your passion is gone, face that sad truth head-on, and don't make any attempts to get it back. Cut your losses and move on. Get divorced quickly, and find a new spouse. Multiple partners are just a reality of the twenty-first century. You're going to live only about eighty years, so don't waste time in a dead marriage. Living without passion is awful, and you deserve better. That fresh burst of passion with your new sweetheart is going to feel marvelous. So, go for it!

Truth: Passion will last in a marriage, if you do it God's way

Secular, popular culture does have two things right in the above myth. First, it is true that every couple's *initial* passion doesn't last. This is infatuation passion, and it always burns out, never to return. Second, culture is correct that losing passion is bad. Catastrophically bad. Marriage is nothing without passion. Loss of passion is boring, draining, destructive, a terrible example for your kids, and not glorifying to God. God does not want you to live together without passion. That's why he put the Song of Solomon in the Bible. Secular culture is, however, tragically and completely *wrong* in two other areas of the above myth.

First, God says passion can be brought back into every marriage. Not infatuation-initial passion—but deep passion. The Song of Solomon delivers this message: "If you put God at the center of your marriage and follow his Passion Principles, you will be rewarded with a heart-thumping, fantastic, passionate love that will last as long as you both shall live."

Second, God says that the marriage bond is sacred, and getting a divorce because of loss of passion is not acceptable. In fact, it will do great damage to you and all those close to you. God wants you to stay married and, by obeying his teaching in the Song, experience deep passion.

Myth #2: Passion Can't Last in a Marriage, but Stay with Your Spouse Anyway (Christian)

You will lose your passion before you reach your twentieth wedding anniversary. In fact, probably a lot sooner than that. But this is perfectly normal and no cause for alarm. Don't panic. Those wonderful, early years of passion are a phase that all couples experience. Your passion gradually leaves and is replaced by a more mature, mellow, and committed love. You know, the kind your great-grandparents have. So, when your passion ends, don't think that there's something wrong with your marriage. Everything's just fine! Your marriage is like a baseball glove that is broken in with use. Or, like a well-worn saddle. God wants you to stay with your spouse and live out your golden years in calmness and peace.

No, it's not too exciting. Yes, the thrill is gone. But that's what marriage is, and you just better get used to it.

Truth: You and your current spouse can experience passion 'til death parts you

It's true that you will lose your *initial* passion. It's not true that you can't get passion back. By inviting God into your marriage and following his Passion Principles, your passion will come roaring back to stay. *True passion is not a phase*

25

of marriage. It is designed by God to be a permanent part of marriage.

It's true that God wants you to stay married. But he certainly does not want you to be in a passion-less marriage. That is not what he has in mind for you. God wants you to feel madly in love, to enjoy exciting sex, and to remain romantic lovers all the way to when you part in death. So—as a matter of fact—your great-grandparents can have this kind of passion.

Myth #3: You Don't Need Passion for a Good Marriage (Christian)

The crazy-in-love passion you feel at the beginning of a romantic relationship is exhilarating, but immature. It burns brightly for a while and then fades. It's good that it fades, because your two hearts simply couldn't stand all that excitement for very long. It's much better to settle down into a solid, stable, comfortable, and responsible love. Love isn't a feeling. It's a rational choice of the will. God isn't concerned about you being happy in your marriage. He just wants you to stay married. Nothing bad will happen if you don't have passion. Your marriage will be routine. Maybe even boring. So what? Your job is to hang in there until one of you dies (of natural causes).

Marriage isn't some kind of never-ending love fest filled with romantic, gushing frivolity. Marriage is serious business. Passion has nothing to do with a good marriage. A good marriage is two persons who choose to stay together no matter how bad and painful the relationship becomes.

Truth: You do need passion for an intimate marriage

Without passion, your marriage will be way below average. Without passion, your marriage has a zero chance to be great. Intimacy cannot exist without passion, and passion is why you're married! A lack of passion can lead to several bad things. The first bad thing is a dead marriage. The second bad thing is the loss of respect and love for your spouse. The third bad thing is each of you will think of and may look for passion outside the marriage.

Everyone has a desperate need for passion. If you don't have it with your spouse, and you are not dedicated to living by biblical principles, you'll try to find it somewhere else: an affair, a sexual addiction, your work, your kids, alcohol, drugs, food, a hobby . . .

How many marriages end because of a lack of passion? Too many to count.

Myth #4: Passion Doesn't Require Any Effort; It Just Happens (Secular, Popular Culture)

Passion is a complete and an utter mystery. It's like magic. Nobody understands why it comes and why it goes. It's natural. It's spontaneous. It's effortless. It explodes between two persons, stays for an indeterminate period of time, and then unpredictably vanishes.

Truth: Passion requires hard work

It's true that the initial attraction and chemistry between two persons is a mystery. Nobody can explain it. But once your initial infatuation wears off, that's when the work begins. *Getting your passion back and keeping it for a lifetime will demand a lot of effort.*

In your temporary infatuation passion, feelings come first and romantic behaviors follow. You "feel" strongly, and therefore you engage in romantic behavior.

When your infatuation passion ceases, you must reverse the process. Now, you must engage in romantic behavior first and then your feelings of passion—deeper and more intimate—will follow.

There is no mystery about the development and maintenance of deep passion. The secular world may not have a clue, but God knows exactly how real passion operates. He reveals these secrets in the Song.

Now, let's take a look at the book of Song of Solomon itself. I need to correct three myths about the Song so you know you can trust its timeless message.

Myth: The Song Is an Allegory

A surprising number of Bible scholars, past and present, cannot accept that God would include a book on romance, sex, and passion in the Bible. So, the Song must only be about something else: God and Israel, Christ and his love for his church, or the relationship between individual Christians and Christ. All the explicitly sexual images in the Song are symbols and metaphors that have nothing to do with literal sex. Their purpose is to teach spiritual principles.

Truth: The Song is the love story of Solomon and Shulamith

The Song is about romance. Passionate love. Sex. That is its central message. The language and terms are explicitly sexual because the book is about sex! If you've never been in a love relationship, I guess you could miss the point of the Song. But there's no excuse for anyone else.

The Song *is* full of symbols and metaphors, but they are all used to tastefully and beautifully describe romance, passion, love, and sex. The Song is clearly and unmistakably about a real man (Solomon), a real woman (Shulamith), and their relationship.

Myth: The Song Is about Young, Idealistic Love

The same persons who believe passion is *only a phase* in a love relationship hold this interpretation of the Song. They say it is a beautiful description of the early years of a young couple who is ecstatically in love. It helps us all as couples to look back with fondness to that bygone era of our relationships when everything was wonderful. However, this type of idealistic, passion-filled love doesn't last, and we all have to move on to a more serious, mature love.

Truth: The Song is about a passionate love that can last and be ended only by death

Yes, the Song is about two lovers during the early years of their relationship. It describes their courtship, wedding, and the first years of their marriage. But the Song's Passion Principles do not apply *only* to the early part of a relationship. God is teaching how to maintain a vibrant, marvelous passion throughout the entire span of a marriage.

Why would God devote an entire book of the Bible to a young, idealistic love that passes quickly and doesn't return? The answer is, he wouldn't! Read Song of Solomon 8:6–7 and tell me what kind of love is being described:

> Place me like a seal over your heart,
> like a seal over your arm;
> for love is as strong as death,
> its jealousy unyielding as the grave.
> It burns like a blazing fire,
> like a mighty flame.

> Many waters cannot quench love;
>   rivers cannot wash it away.
> If one were to give all the wealth of his house for love,
>   it would be utterly scorned.

A *seal* indicates permanence. Being as strong as *death* indicates permanence. *Waters* and *rivers* can't wash this love away. Why? Because it is permanent. It lasts the lifetimes of the spouses.

Myth: Solomon Is Not Qualified to Write about True Love

Be serious. I mean, come on. We're talking about the ultimate playboy. Talk about a womanizer! The man had three hundred wives and seven hundred concubines! How could a moral degenerate like Solomon have anything to say about a passionate, permanent love between one man and one woman? Maybe he could write a book about how to get more chicks, but not one about genuine love.

Truth: God chose Solomon to write the ultimate book about real love

Two truths about Solomon that are stated in the Bible should be kept in mind. (1) Regarding his sins, the *consequences* for his sins later in life were immense. One huge, tragic, historical result was God's taking the kingdom of Israel from Solomon's son and the division of the kingdom (1 Kings 11:9–13) and the eventual fall of both divisions. (2) Regarding his wisdom, God told Solomon, "Ask what you wish Me to give you" (1 Kings 3:4). In response to Solomon's request, God gave him "a wise and discerning heart, so that there has been no one like you before you, nor shall one like you arise after you" (1 Kings 3:12). From *his divinely appointed wisdom* came 3,000 proverbs and 1,005 songs (1 Kings 4:32). And out of the wisdom with which God blessed him came this book of love.

Solomon also wrote Ecclesiastes and Proverbs, two books of incredible wisdom about life and relationships. Are we going to doubt the truth in these books because of Solomon's sexual sins? I don't think so.

God revealed to Solomon the truth about marriage: one man and one woman, God at the center, all their lives. God chose to use this flawed man to write the world's most powerful how-to manual on love and passion in marriage. Despite Solomon's terrible sexual sins, the Song is the God-breathed truth about how to get deep passion in marriage and how to keep it. That's why it's in the Bible. Here's the bottom line about passion and the Song:

> Your initial infatuation passion leaves. You can get your passion back and this time it will be a deeper and much more intimate passion. The Song will tell you how.

And, because it's God's way, it's guaranteed to work!

3

"Even the Dog Is More Important Than I Am!"

Scientists tell us that black holes are one of the most powerful and frightening forces in the universe. They are vast, voracious vacuums that suck everything near them into their gaping mouths. Stars, planets, and even galaxies, even light itself, cannot withstand their mighty gravitational pull. And whatever is swallowed by these horrible black holes is gone forever.

I'm not afraid of black holes. Not in the least. If I were in outer space, next to a black hole, I'd laugh in its face. I'd say, "Hey, is that all you've got? You'll have to try a little harder! Bring it on!" You see, I've lived for years with four black holes: my four kids. I love my kids dearly. But their amazing sucking power has no equal in the universe. If you have kids, you know what I'm talking about. I'll bet you can relate to the following brief overview of the parenting process.

There is one question that has haunted parents for centuries. Here it is: are children gifts from God, or instruments of slow torture? Actually, they are both. Parenting has moments of wonder, excitement, and enrichment—broken up by long stretches of exasperation, total chaos, and suffering.

As you begin parenthood with a newborn, you just want this little person to survive. You sneak into the nursery every thirty minutes to make sure the little thing is still breathing. You meet every need of this small, helpless creature.

When your child hits the twos and threes and is systematically destroying your home—piece by broken piece—you begin to wonder if *you* will survive.

When your child moves into junior high and becomes a teenager, you know you're not going to make it. You realize with horror that the roles are reversed. You are now a small, helpless creature at the mercy of a far superior force: hormones.

If you and your ungrateful, hostile, and attitude-challenged teenager survive through high school, two things will happen. One, your health is broken. Two, you must now spend your retirement savings on college. Talk about a gamble! All that money for a kid you're not even sure is going to turn out well. With your health broken and your money spent, you must spend your declining years praying that one of your kids will have pity on you and take care of you. That's the reason Sandy and I had four kids. We figure at least one of them will look after us when we're in our wheelchair years.

The Big Six

Our children are precious to us. They also demand huge amounts of time, attention, energy, and money. Because of this, it is very easy to neglect your spouse as you attempt to meet the all-consuming needs of your children.

Kids are one of what I call The Big Six: persons and activities that can sneak ahead of your spouse on your priority list. Read my description of The Big Six below, and be honest about which of them *you* are making *more important* than your marriage partner.

Your Kids

Raise your hand if you are placing your kids above your spouse. Go ahead, don't be ashamed. You have a lot of company. My wife Sandy and I spent years making this mistake. The cold, hard reality of a child-centered home hit me between my sleep-deprived eyes one fateful night.

My lovely wife and I were sound asleep. It was the middle of the night. Suddenly, I sensed the presence of someone by my bedside. I cracked open an eye to take a look. Was it a burglar? No. I almost wished it had been. At least that would have been a good reason to be roused out of the few paltry hours of sleep I struggled to get each night.

It was one of my daughters, of course. She'll remain nameless for her own protection. I immediately closed my eye and pretended to be asleep, hoping that Sandy would be forced to deal with the little intruder. What a waste of time that was. Sandy said, "Nice try, you weasel. She came to your side. She loves her daddy. So, Daddy can handle her."

My daughter and I engaged in this wonderful dialogue:

Daughter: "I'm scared."
Dad: "No, I'm scared. I'm scared I won't be able to get back to sleep."
Daughter: "There's a monster in my room."

Dad: "I'm not sure what's worse, a monster in your room or a kid in mine. Maybe you can ask the monster for help."

Daughter: "I can't sleep."

Dad: "Really? Neither can I, now."

Daughter: "I think my bed is wet."

Dad: "No, honey, we're past the think stage. I can tell by the smell. It's wet."

Daughter: "I need water."

Dad: "Your bed is wet, and you want water? I don't think so."

Desperate for some help or—at the very least—some show of moral support, I nudged Sandy. She said, "What? What are you looking at? I gave birth to that kid and it hurt, a lot. It won't hurt you nearly as much to change her bed and get her some clean pajamas." And then my wonderful wife rolled over and returned to her blissful sleep.

Right at that moment, in the middle of the night, I had my marital epiphany. In a loud voice, I screeched: "These kids are killing us!" Our daughter didn't understand it, and I don't think Sandy even heard it. But I meant it.

I realized that our relationship was all about the kids. As a psychologist, I had counseled hundreds of parents to not allow their marriages to become child-centered. Too bad I wasn't following my own advice. Sandy and I were as child centered as you can get.

When working with traditional as well as blended families, I can't tell you how many times parents have told me, "My kids are more important to me than my spouse." "I love my kids more than my spouse." I ask them to show me where it says in the Bible that children are more important than a spouse. Of course, they can't do it.

It doesn't make any difference if your spouse is your first or your third. Your spouse is more important than your kids! If you focus too much on your kids, you'll hurt your marriage. You'll end up just parents and not lovers. If you focus too much on your kids, you'll hurt *them*. They'll learn by your example how to build a mediocre marriage.

Your Job

"I'm working for you and the kids."

"I have to establish myself in my career."

"I'm preparing for our retirement."

"Long hours just come with the job."

"Hey, if I don't work this hard, we don't eat."

"I'll be home more when things lighten up."

Sound familiar? These are the words of a workaholic. I ought to know, because I'm a workaholic. I've used all these statements with Sandy in the past. They are all rationalizations to cover up the nasty truth: you are an addict, and your drive to produce and succeed at work has nothing to do with your spouse or your kids. It's all about you.

Men tend to be more guilty of this, but I've seen plenty of female work addicts as well. Stop kidding yourself. If you are placing your job above your spouse, you are killing your love. Most of your time and energy and creativity are being spent at work. So what happens to your marriage? It withers from neglect.

Your Home

You're the kind of person who just can't sit still and relax in your own home. Not when there are jobs to do. And there are always jobs to do. You have ants in your pants!

You're always moving, always doing, and always puttering. You feel good when you are completing jobs and being productive.

You can't stand to leave any job undone. Although there are men who fit this category, it's usually the woman who focuses too much on the household chores. You think you simply have to complete all the daily jobs—laundry, dishes, food preparation, vacuuming, dusting, grocery shopping, cleaning the bathrooms, making the beds, paying the bills, watering the lawn, picking up clutter—before you can spend time with your spouse.

You're the kind of person who is damaging your marriage. You don't mean to, but you are. You're acting as if a clean and orderly home is to be more highly prized than a great, intimate marriage. That's absurd, isn't it? Yes, it is! The household jobs have to get done. But not before you meet the needs of your spouse.

Hobbies

Are your hobbies above your wife or husband on the priority list? Men are particularly guilty of this marital crime. Television. Sports on television. Sports outside the home. Golf. Hunting. Fishing. The computer. Video games. The gym. Do you have any idea how it feels to know your husband values his fun activities more than you? It feels pretty lousy. In fact, very lousy.

Many husbands believe that simply being together in the same geographical space is "quality time." Using this reasoning, husbands figure they can do their fun activity and still make their wives happy. Watching a television show in the den or bedroom is quality time. Reading the paper at the kitchen table is quality time. Working on the computer while she reads a book is quality time. No, it's not. You might as well be in different homes in different states, because there is no connection.

A husband and a wife ride in the car together for forty-five minutes with absolutely no conversation. The husband thinks, "Hey, that was a great trip. We were together, and I enjoyed it. I wish I could have caught a few more green lights." His wife thinks, "Our marriage is over. We have nothing to talk about. He hates me. He's probably already seen a divorce attorney."

The truth is, your spouse needs to feel more important than your hobbies. A healthy marriage requires conversation, not just being in each other's company.

The wife needs her husband's eye contact, his complete attention, and a decent conversation in which personal things are shared. And, she needs this experience on a regular basis. Although he's usually not aware of it, the husband has the same need.

Your Pets

The husband sat on my office couch next to his wife and said, "Dr. Clarke, I have solid evidence that another male is more important to my wife than I am." His wife was shocked and stammered, "What . . . what do you mean? That's not true!" He calmly looked at her and said, "Yeah? What about Buddy?" She laughed out loud and said, "Buddy is our dog!" He replied, "Exactly, my dear."

The husband spent the next ten minutes describing how he'd been replaced by Buddy. (I couldn't resist saying, "No longer the top dog, huh?") "Doc, when she comes home in the evening, she goes right to Buddy: 'How's my little man? Mommy loves you so much. Mommy missed you today. Let me kiss your face and hug you, you sweet furball!' After a few minutes of loving on Buddy, she gives me a peck on the cheek. The rest of the evening I have to watch as a four-footed mongrel gets most of the love and attention from my wife. Buddy gets fed before me. Buddy gets more kisses, more hugs, and more massages than I do. She says many more sweet, loving, and complimentary things to Buddy. When Buddy has a urinary accident, she's very patient and kind with him. When I make a mess or forget to do a chore, she's impatient and critical.

"Doc, the dog is more important than me! I want to be Buddy because he's closer to my wife than I am. The other night, I came to bed late and found Buddy sleeping next to my wife on my side of the bed! I half expected him to be wearing my pajamas! I shook him awake and he actually growled at me. By the look in his eyes, I could have sworn he was thinking, 'I'm taking over, loser. Sleep on the couch.'"

I've seen this kind of overkill pet devotion happen with dogs, cats, ferrets, birds, and hamsters. When a pet gets more time, attention, affection, and communication than your spouse, something's wrong! Actually, *someone's* wrong. You!

Your Family and Friends

A husband continues to hang out with his single friends at their homes. His wife feels neglected, but he says, "Getting married shouldn't mean I have to give up all my friends." When you add it up, he spends more time each week with his friends than he does with his wife.

A wife spends, on average, an hour and a half on the telephone or online with family and friends each evening. While she talks and talks, her husband watches television or reads. She is closer emotionally to her "buddies" than she is to her own husband.

A husband calls his mother at least three times a week. He relies on her for praise, encouragement, and advice. He talks to her about issues and decisions in his life before he talks to his wife. He does whatever he can to please his mother. He does what she tells him to do. When his mother and his wife have a different opinion about something, he sides with Mom. He's a mama's boy and is rapidly losing the respect of his wife.

A wife has never really broken away from her father, become her own person. She is used to relying on his wisdom and guidance and continues to depend heavily on him. Her husband wants to be the leader and for them to make decisions together, but she insists upon calling Dad to get his input. It's time for her to stop being Daddy's little girl.

A married couple is in a close-knit social group of couples. They go out with this group at least once a week and sometimes more often. It's a lot of fun, but this couple's relationship isn't as close as it used to be. They're having trouble finding things to talk about when it's just the two of them. They are finding it more comfortable and more enjoyable to be with their friends.

First Things First

Every one of The Big Six is important and can add value and meaning to life. Nevertheless, not one of them is as important as your marriage.

When your spouse isn't your top priority, your marriage automatically becomes less and less intimate. You don't want that to happen, but it does happen. You slowly but surely pull apart and you experience a breakdown in these critical areas:

You have very little personal, one-on-one time together.
You have no regular, intimate communication.

You don't meet each other's real physical, emotional, and spiritual needs.

If anyone or anything is more important than your spouse is, your marriage cannot be deeply intimate and passionate. That's for sure. Your relationship will slip to good, pretty good, mediocre, and then poor. Finally, your love will die.

What's the solution to the damaging effects of The Big Six? It's in the Song.

4

"You're My Number One, Baby!"

I hate Ted. I've always hated Ted. I don't believe there will ever come a day when I don't hate Ted. "Who is Ted?" you ask, "and what did he do to you?" I'll tell you who Ted is. Ted is the guy who dated Sandy in high school. That's right. Ted was my beautiful wife's boyfriend back in the 1970s.

You're thinking, "So what? Was Ted a jerk? Did he mistreat Sandy in any way?" No. Actually, he was a great Christian guy who treated her very well. His crime was (and remains to this day) having an exclusive, close relationship with Sandy. Just the thought of any other guy, even thirty years ago, being close to my Sandy makes me cringe.

You see, Sandy is the most important person in my life and has been ever since we met in 1978. I am jealous, in a healthy way, of my relationship with this remarkable woman. She is my best friend. She is my confidant. She is my lover. She is my soul mate. I don't want anyone to be closer to her than me. So, I hate Ted. If you're reading this, Ted, I'm sorry. But, I'll bet you hate your wife's old boyfriends too.

Do you think I'm into a little overkill here? Too intense? Out of line? No, I'm not. And I can prove it. Solomon and Shulamith feel the same way I do.

You're the Best!

The Song of Solomon teaches that your spouse is your number one human priority.

> Solomon (2:2)
> "Like a lily among the thorns,
> So is my darling among the maidens."

Solomon says Shulamith is a lily, and all the other women are thorns. They are not even other flowers. Thorns! She is not one beautiful woman among many beautiful women. No. She is the most beautiful woman in the world, by far. No other woman is even close!

> Shulamith (2:3)
> "Like an apple tree among the trees of the forest,
> So is my beloved among the young men."

Shulamith, not to be outdone, says Solomon is an apple tree and all the other guys are just regular, run-of-the-mill trees. An apple tree is much better than a plain, old tree, because it provides shade, comfort, and nourishment.

Shulamith (5:10)

"My beloved is dazzling and ruddy,

Outstanding among ten thousand."

Her man is dazzling! That's pretty high praise. When Shulamith uses the word outstanding, she is referring to Solomon's character. As a man of character and integrity, she wants him to know he has no equal.

Solomon (6:8–9)

"There are sixty queens and eighty concubines,

And maidens without number;

But my dove, my perfect one, is unique . . ."

Perfect? Oh, come on! Nobody's perfect! Wrong. Solomon says Shulamith is perfect, and he's not exaggerating. He means it. He wants to convince his wife that she is the absolute best, one of a kind, and far superior in every way to every other woman. He's not saying he doesn't notice other women. He's saying they can't hold a candle to his woman.

Peel Yourself Off the Big Six

Your spouse is more important than everyone and everything else in your life. To make this biblical truth a reality, peel yourself off whomever and whatever is above your spouse. Give your spouse permission to tell you—anytime—when he or she does not feel like the top priority in your life. Your response to any such expression ought to be, "You're right. I'm sorry. How can I make you feel and know you are the priority in my life?" Then, do what your spouse asks you to do.

45

Best Friends

Great passion cannot exist without great friendship. In their Song of love, Solomon and Shulamith live out this truth. They are, unquestionably, best friends.

From 4:9–5:2, Solomon calls Shulamith "my sister" five times. It is a term of intense affection and indicates that he considers their relationship to be as close as brother and sister. It is as if they are bonded by blood.

Shulamith (5:16)

"This is my beloved and this is my friend,

O daughters of Jerusalem."

Shulamith wants others to know that Solomon is more than the man she loves. He is also her friend. In fact, I don't believe that you become beloved without also being a friend.

In 5:1, God seems to confirm the lovers' deep, rich friendship by calling them "friends." He does this, interestingly enough, at the same time they are experiencing sexual intercourse for the first time.

Tell Me First

One simple way to cultivate best friend status in your marriage is to always share your life experiences first with your spouse. As you go through your day, all kinds of things happen to you. Routine things. Funny things. Interesting things. Painful things. Stressful things. Spiritual things. Even zany things. Save these personal events and let your spouse be the first one to hear them.

If you blab to others before sharing with your spouse, you water down the impact of your experiences. Your thoughts and emotions get diluted and lose their vibrancy. When you share something, it has much more punch the first time you share it. You and your first-time listener form an emotional, relational bond that subsequent retellings cannot produce.

If you want to tell others later, fine. Let them get less punch and less bonding. Let your spouse get the original, fresh version when you and your emotions are deeper and more spontaneous. This way, the two of you have a better chance to connect at the heart level and branch off into a great conversation.

Make Time and Talk

A common misconception about the Song is that it's all about sex—you know, a lot of kissing, touching, and intercourse going on. And, believe me, a lot of this kind of erotic, physical behavior does go on in the book. (More on the physical in later chapters.)

But the Song is filled with passages on communication and emotional connection. God, through Solomon and Shulamith, is telling us that regular, intimate conversations prepare lovers for great, passionate sex.

Shulamith (2:3)
"In his shade I took great delight and sat down,
And his fruit was sweet to my taste."

Shulamith is with Solomon in a private place. She feels safe and protected with him. She is praising his speech and saying that she is getting to know him intimately. She is delighting in their deepening communication. The two sweethearts will soon enjoy physical intimacy, but they prepare for physical closeness with emotional closeness.

Solomon (2:14)

"O my dove, in the clefts of the rock,
In the secret place of the steep pathway,
Let me see your form,
Let me hear your voice;
For your voice is sweet,
And your form is lovely."

Solomon has made time to be alone with Shulamith. They are together in a secluded place. It is not a time to get physical. Not yet. It is a time to get emotionally connected. He wants to be with her, to see her, and to hear her talk. He wants to get to know her. He admires her beauty, but it's not only about her physical beauty here. He desires to know her more deeply as a person. This is a time to focus on her and listen to her.

Wouldn't every wife love to have her husband do what Solomon is doing here? Wouldn't your wife be thrilled with this kind of a private conversation time in your home? You'd better believe she would!

Talk This Way

Schedule at least four thirty-minute couple talks per week. Sit down every weekend and schedule these talk times. Schedule two weeks ahead if necessary. If you can get more than four a week, great. But get at least four. (For help in learning how to talk to each other, see my book, *Cinderella Meets the Caveman*.)

Here are some specific how-tos for your couple talk times:

When

The time of day doesn't matter. You can talk in the morning, midday, or in the evening. If you talk in the evening, do it as early in the evening as possible. You need to talk when you're still fairly fresh and have some brain cells operating. Don't try to communicate at the end of the evening when you both are tired.

Get your crumb-crunching black holes—um, kids—to bed or out of your hair, so you can have complete privacy. I know you love your kids. God loves your kids. The whole world loves your kids. But you need to remove them from your presence so you can build intimacy in your talk times.

Kids are never mentioned in the Song. You want to know why? Because where kids are, romance and passion die! That's why! Your marriage is your number one human priority in life, and you need kid-free talk times.

Where

Choose a talking place in your home that is private and quiet. You are creating an oasis in the middle of your busy, stressful lives. It's an escape into your relationship. No children, no television, no computer, no telephones—cell or any other kind—no pets, and no newspapers or magazines. No distractions. Period.

Make your talking place warm, soft, and inviting. The ambience can make a real difference. You're creating a mood. The deeper the mood, the deeper the conversation will be. Turn the lights down low, play some soothing music in the background, and have a candle or two burning.

How

Okay, you have your wonderful children in their rooms. You are sitting together in your talk time place. What now? I recommend you follow my five-step couple talk time plan. These five progressive steps will lead you gradually to intimacy. This plan has worked for Sandy and me for years. It has worked for hundreds of couples I've seen in my therapy office. It will work for you too.

First step: Start with a brief prayer

Take each other's hands and say a short prayer: "Thank you, Lord, for giving us each other. Thank you for this time together. Please help us to open up and really connect in conversation. Amen." That's it. Thirty seconds, at the most. This prayer deepens the mood and invites God into the process.

Second step: Read your couple's devotional

Read a page from a couple's devotional and answer the questions at the end. It's easy and a great conversation starter. Two excellent resources are the Dobsons' *Night Light*, and the Raineys' *Moments Together for Couples*. The devotional gets you warmed up and could trigger a stimulating conversation.

Third step: What's on your mind?

Here, you each suggest daily living topics like, what happened today, work, family and friends, spiritual life, church, stresses, worries, and events that triggered strong emotions. You're catching up on your lives and looking for a topic or two that show potential for more intimacy.

When you find a promising topic, talk about it, and agree to continue talking about it at your next talk time. I call these "carry-over topics." Talking about the same topic two, three, or four times will create a deeper level of emotional intimacy.

Fourth step: Pray together

You're going to have a longer—five or ten minutes—prayer time now. Get a pad and make a list of prayer requests. Divide the list between you and pray for the requests one at a time, back and forth. Hold hands when you pray, because this creates a mood and connects you via touch.

Fifth step: Move from prayer to conversation

When you finish praying, talk about some of the things you just lifted to God in prayer. These are the concerns of your heart, the important persons and situations you care about the most. These form your *bridge* from prayer to conversation between you.

This progression is not set in concrete. I know it works, especially for couples who are just beginning to have talk times. Give it a try. Play with the order of the steps. Mix them. Find a sequence that works best for you as a couple.

Meet Needs

One of the ways Solomon and Shulamith practice priority in their relationship is by meeting each other's most important needs. Shulamith meets Solomon's need to be respected and honored (5:10). She also meets his need to be desired sexually (5:16). Respect, honor, and sex are three of nearly every husband's most important needs.

Solomon meets Shulamith's need to be loved unconditionally and completely (2:14). He meets her need to be provided for, to be protected, and to feel secure (3:6–11). He leads her in communication and meets her need to be emotionally connected to him (4:1–10). Nearly every wife would list unconditional love, protection and security, and emotional connection, in her list of top five needs.

You Gotta Ask

The only surefire, guaranteed way to identify your spouse's needs is to ask. Don't assume you know. Don't try to read your partner's mind. At least twice a day, ask, in person or over the telephone, what his or her needs are.

Ask in the morning, before you go your separate ways: "Honey, what are your needs today? What can I do for you?" Husband, because you don't have a memory, jot down your wife's needs. At the beginning of your evening together, when you first see each other, ask for each other's needs again. "Sweetheart, what can I do for you tonight?"

Once a week, in one of your talk times, ask your spouse: "How am I doing meeting your needs? How can I do better?" When needs are not met, passion erodes. So, get a need-meeting performance evaluation once a week.

Solomon and Shulamith have a love that is intense. Bordering on obsessive. It is clearly the most important part of their lives. They know the secret of *priority*. They make each other number one. And, boy, does it pay off in passion!

5

The Sheet Hog
and the Mad Snorter

Sandy Clarke is a sheet hog. There, I've said it. After twenty-five years of keeping her dirty little secret, it feels good to finally expose the truth. By day, Sandy is a wonderful wife and mother. She is a selfless, nurturing, and kind servant who focuses on the needs of others. But, by night, she turns into a selfish, grasping, and greedy sheet hog.

I need a crisp, clean sheet covering my vulnerable body. Do you know the purpose of a sheet? It regulates body temperature during the night. It keeps you feeling cool and fresh so you can sleep soundly. It acts as a barrier between your body and the heavier, more abrasive blanket. Everybody needs a sheet! Everybody is entitled to a sheet!

Every night, Sandy and I start with the sheet evenly distributed across our bodies. We're both happy. The sheet belongs to both of us. We're a team. We're sharing. I kiss her goodnight, and we drift off to sleep. My last conscious thought is, "Maybe tonight I'll get to keep my half of the sheet."

Every night—and I'm not exaggerating—I wake up between one and two a.m. with no sheet. Sandy has stolen—that's right, stolen—the entire sheet! She is literally rolled up in the sheet. It's like sleeping with a mummy. The sheet is wrapped around her body and securely wedged under her. It would take the Jaws of Life to get it off her. And don't think I haven't considered that option.

Even if I could somehow unwind the sheet, it wouldn't do me any good. The top of the sheet is all bunched up near her beautiful face, and she has a death grip on it with both her hands. She's not giving up that sheet!

What do I do? All you spouses who sleep with a Sheet Hog know what I do. I grab that sheet and yank it as hard as I can, which spins Sandy around and breaks her control of the sheet. As I yank, I yell in a Tarzan-like voice, "I'm taking back my half of the sheet, Sheet Hog!"

I wish I had the guts to do that. I've often fantasized about it. But, I don't. You sheetless spouses know what I do. I do nothing. I take it like a man. I go without the sheet for the rest of the night. Without that sheet, I'm exposed to the elements, and the ceiling fan makes me cold. If I pull the blanket over me, it's scratchy and makes me hot.

I'm uncomfortable. I'm out of sorts. I have trouble going back to sleep. As I toss and turn, I'm forced to watch Sandy as she sleeps like a baby. With my half of the sheet helping her sleep.

Is Sandy apologetic for her sheet hogging or in any way concerned about it? Shockingly, no, she is not. She always laughs when I bring it up, as though it's some kind of a joke. I asked her to go to some kind of sleep laboratory where a minor but painful shock would be administered each time she began her sheet hogging behavior. She refused. In fact, her exact words were, "In your dreams, *Mad Snorter!*"

Why would Sandy call me a Mad Snorter? Well, I have a confession to make. Sandy is not the only one with an obnoxious, annoying nighttime behavior. I snore. And if snoring isn't bad enough, I snort. Loudly. Several times a night.

Just about every night, I'm sleeping—actually, snoring—and suddenly I rip off a massive, big-bang, ear-splitting snort. It's so loud I wake myself up. And Sandy. And the kids. And the little dog two houses down the street.

The first few times it happened, I said to Sandy, "What was that? Did a car backfire? Did someone fire a shotgun?" I was serious! I had no idea it was me. Sandy said, "It was you, Mad Snorter!" She had the nerve to be upset, lying there all wrapped up in my sheet.

Sandy told me she could probably handle my snoring, but my snorting was a problem. My huge snorts woke her up at least twice a night. I tried to convince her my snorts were my body's way of reacting to the trauma of not having the sheet. I said, "It's as if my body is crying out, 'I have no sheet. Help me!'" Sandy didn't buy it.

Being a good husband, I tried all kinds of snoring remedies. Adhesive strips on my nose. Pills. Magnets. All kinds of special pillows. I even used one pillow filled with buckwheat hulls. It felt as though I were sleeping on a pillow filled with, well . . . buckwheat hulls.

I still snort. Sandy has assured me she won't divorce me because of my snoring. Suffocation is a possibility, but not divorce. Sandy still hogs the sheet. I have accepted the brutal reality that I will sleep the rest of my life without a sheet.

You know what? That's okay. It's better than okay. Why? Because I get to live with the most wonderful person in the world. Yes, Sandy is a Sheet Hog. But her many positive qualities far outweigh her sheet hogging. Sandy feels the same about me. I am a nocturnal snorter, but Sandy chooses to dwell on my many strengths.

We have learned that focusing on each other's weaknesses and imperfections weakens our marriage. So, we deliberately determine every day to concentrate on positives and not negatives.

Making Molehills into Mountains

Many spouses make the mistake of allowing small annoyances to turn into federal cases. The molehills of bad habits and irritating behaviors that were overlooked early in the relationship can grow into mountains of intolerance and resentment. The husband begins to focus more and more on the negative traits of his wife. And the wife does the same thing with her husband.

All this negativity sucks the joy and love right out of the relationship. Appreciation of the positives that got you married in the first place fade away. The spontaneity and thrill of passion is replaced by the dullness and frustration of resentment.

When I see a married couple in therapy, my initial job is to get the spouses to stop the negative flow and start a positive flow. Let me tell you, it's a tough job. Each partner is zeroed in on the faults of the other, and the blame game is in full swing.

When I tell husbands and wives their first assignment is to write a letter detailing *their own faults* in the marriage, they are horrified. I'm met with stunned silence which quickly turns into protestations of "but our problems are my spouse's fault."

In over twenty-one years of seeing couples in therapy, I have heard just about every marital complaint you could possibly imagine. Here's a brief list including my comments to the complaining spouse. I think you'll recognize most of these. (And, yes, I am trying to make you feel guilty.)

"She's Overweight!"

Husband: "Doc, I'm just not physically attracted to my wife anymore. We've had two kids, and her body isn't the same as when we got married. The extra weight she's carrying is a real turn-off. I have never been attracted to overweight women. I don't want to make love to her. Frankly, I don't even like being around her. I have brought up her weight a number of times, and each time she's gotten very angry and hurt. She runs crying to our bedroom, and I feel like the bad guy."

Dave Clarke: "You ought to feel like the bad guy, because you are the bad guy. You moron! When was the last time you looked in the mirror? You're not exactly male model material. You might be able to model underwear for a store called *Big, Paunchy, and Out of Shape. We* didn't have two kids, either. *She* gave birth to those babies. Pregnancy changes a woman's body. Let's put an eight-pound bowling ball in your belly, have you carry it around for nine months, and then squeeze it between your legs. I'll bet your hips will change too. Your critical comments are destroying her self-esteem and her love for you. She already feels inadequate compared to all those glamorous, surgically enhanced babes in the media. Now, you've convinced her that she's ugly. Go home, fall on your knees, and beg her forgiveness. I'd throw in some serious groveling while you're at it. Then tell her often she's beautiful. In time, she will gain confidence."

"He's a Lazy Bum!"

Wife: "I can't seem to get my husband to do much of anything around the house. He works hard and makes a good living, but I do ninety percent of the household chores. What drives me batty is he'll promise to do a chore but then won't do it. He'll tell me, 'I'll do it later,' but later never comes. He forgets, and I end up doing it. I refuse to let him get away with being a slacker. I keep after him every day, asking him to do jobs and pointing out the jobs he hasn't done. I get pretty sharp with him, but I feel like I have to light a fire under him. He says, 'I can't please you,' but that's a cop out."

Dave Clarke: "You are a world-class nag. I'm sure you don't want to be, but you are. You're pecking him to death. It's a form of torture. A man never responds to that kind of treatment. He's a slacker at home. You're right. But continually criticizing him won't motivate him. His feeling that he can't please you is real. When a man believes he can't win, he quits trying. Plus, being a nag makes you miserable. Start praising him for his hard work at his job. Praise him for every job he does around the house. Praise him for the character qualities in him you admire. When he's praised regularly, he'll be a happier husband and inclined to be more helpful."

"She's a Lousy Housekeeper!"

Husband: "You would not believe how disorganized my wife is. She can't seem to handle her responsibilities at home. Every evening, I come home to chaos. The house is a mess, the kids' toys are everywhere, the kids' homework isn't done, and she's running behind on dinner. I get angry, because I know the answer is self discipline and time management. I tell her that she has plenty of time to complete all her tasks. I mean, the kids are in school most of the day! If I had the time she has, the home would run efficiently."

Dave Clarke: "Sir, I don't think you'd last a day if you changed roles with your wife. Do you have any idea what it's like juggling all the household chores with the kids in your hair? You'd be begging for your mamma by the end of the first day. Even if you could be more efficient than she is, that's not the point. She's your wife, and she is a wonderful person with many great qualities. Stop crabbing about what she's *not* doing and start complimenting her for what she *is* doing. You didn't marry her because of her tremendous housekeeping and time management skills. You married her because you love her. Also, get off your duff and help her with the chores and the kids."

"He Drives Like a Maniac!"

Wife: "My husband thinks he's a race car driver on the road. He's always in a terrible hurry. He drives too fast, he's impatient, and he cuts in and out of traffic like a madman. He continually honks at other drivers and calls them names when they're too slow to satisfy him or they impede his progress in any way. I'm glad we don't have a

Christian bumper sticker on our car. I'm always telling him to relax, to slow down, and to be more careful. Just about every car ride is ruined because of all the tension and conflict between us."

Dave Clarke: "You married a man, that's your problem. Peppering him with warnings and criticizing his driving won't change him. It will only damage your relationship. For him and most guys, every car ride is a NASCAR race. He's in a competition to get where he's going as quickly as possible. You could have married a man who is sweet, kind, nice, and drives like a ninety-nine-year-old woman. You didn't do that. You married a regular guy."

Flaws, Quirks, Pet Peeves, and Other Assorted Imperfections

He leaves his clothes on the floor. She has too many clothes but keeps buying more. He refuses to stop putting his socks and shirts into the laundry inside out. She talks on the phone too much. He stalls and stalls on doing home improvement projects. She won't sit with me and watch television. All he does is sit on his keister all weekend watching sports on television. She spends way too much time cleaning the house. He smacks his lips when he's eating. She clicks her teeth. He picks his nails. She cracks her knuckles. He wears old, worn out, food-stained clothes. She has the world's biggest shoe collection. He belches and won't say "excuse me." She hogs the bathroom and uses up all the hot water. He won't replace the toilet paper. She takes up ninety percent of our closet. He has bad breath. She's always late. He leaves his whiskers in the sink after shaving.

Do any of these complaints sound familiar? I could go on and on and on. Living with a member of the opposite sex brings out all kinds of annoying behaviors. It is easy—very easy—to begin focusing on your partner's negative qualities. If the pattern continues, your view of your spouse becomes all or mostly negative.

It's not the annoying behaviors themselves that cause the damage to the marriage. Most of them are not that big a deal. It's your *focus* on these behaviors that causes the damage. The positives are eliminated and you are left with only the negatives. Your love cannot and will not survive under these circumstances. Nitpicking negativity is one of Satan's most effective tools for destroying a marriage.

I'm not saying that these kind of annoying, irritating behaviors don't ever need to be addressed. Some need to be ignored, but some need to be changed. What I'm saying is that you must not allow your spouse's flaws to outnumber your spouse's good qualities in your mind. Also, when you begin to deliberately insert positive comments and compliments, watch how they squeeze out the negatives.

When you and your mate are maintaining a huge, regular flow of positives, that's when negatives and weaknesses can be tackled and fixed.

Solomon and Shulamith did not complain about each other's imperfections. Quite the opposite.

6 ·

"You're the Most Wonderful Person in the World"

Some time ago, I saw a couple in their fifties in marital therapy. When I came out to my lobby to meet them before their first session, they were sitting on opposite sides of the room. Not a good sign. It became clear quite soon that they hated each other's guts. The atmosphere in my therapy office was thick with their mutual resentment and bitterness.

They told me their story, and it was an ugly one. Multiple affairs. Domestic violence. Bitter disagreements over money and parenting. Verbal abuse. Chronic, nasty conflict over a wide variety of petty issues. At least sex wasn't a problem: they hadn't had sex for twenty years. They slept in separate bedrooms.

About halfway through the session, I thought to myself: "This is one of the worst marriages I've ever seen." At the end of the session, when it was time to give my evaluation, I said, "I have to be honest with you. Your marriage is awful. Unbelievably bad. It's not even a marriage. It's more of an ongoing feud. But with God's help and hard work, your marriage can be fixed. It can be a great marriage. The first step is to create some positive flow in your relationship."

I stepped to my huge window, opened the blinds, and said, "As you can see, this window has a complete view of the parking lot. I'll be standing here watching, and I want to see you holding hands as you walk to your car. If you're not holding hands, I will rap on the window."

If looks could kill, I would have been murdered on the spot. I thought for one frantic moment they weren't going to pay me. They thought I was crazy, and they told me so. But they did it! As I watched, they held hands on the way to their car. It was awkward and forced for the first ten steps, but then something clicked, and I could tell they were enjoying it. There was a spark of life between them. This couple had a lot of hard work to do over the next three months of therapy, but the change in their marriage began with the simple act of holding hands.

Solomon and Shulamith would love this story. It illustrates a truth about marriage that they live out in the Song: Positives Produce Passion.

Praise, Praise, and More Praise

The positives in the Song come in the form of verbal praise. A lot of it. Solomon and Shulamith aren't shy about complimenting each other. They are effusive in their praise. They quite literally *gush* over each other's positive qualities. Why? Because they know this results in passion. And passion is what they want!

Over and over in the Song, the same progression is illustrated by the two lovers: praise first, followed by passion.

"Kiss Me, Mr. Olive Oil"

Shulamith (1:2–3)

> "May he kiss me with the kisses of his mouth!
> For your love is better than wine.
> Your oils have a pleasing fragrance,
> Your name is like purified oil . . ."

Shulamith wants his wonderful kisses. She praises his love and compares him to pure olive oil. In that day, olive oil was rare and precious. She is complimenting him on his purity and goodness.

Shulamith (1:4)

> "Draw me after you and let us run together!
> The king has brought me into his chambers."

Chambers? What are they going to do in his chambers? Play checkers? Read the paper? Fold the laundry? No! Shulamith praises him, and then she wants him physically.

"You Are So Beautiful, I Can't Stand It"

The woman always wants the details. She wants to know—indeed, needs to know—why you feel the way you do about her.

Husband: "I love you, honey."
Wife: "Why?"
Husband: "What do you mean, why? I just do."

Sound like a familiar dialogue? Your wife wants to hear the specific reasons behind your love for her. She wants to hear the qualities about her that make her lovable. She's looking for reassurance, and when she gets the specifics, that locks it in for her. Now she can really believe you love her and see her as beautiful.

Solomon knows Shulamith needs to hear the details of his feelings for her. In 4:1–7, he paints a verbal portrait of the most beautiful woman in the world. It is his woman, Shulamith.

Solomon (4:1a)

"How beautiful you are, my darling,
How beautiful you are!"

A good beginning. He calls her beautiful twice. Most husbands would stop right there. Not Solomon. He's just getting warmed up.

Solomon (4:1b)

"Your eyes are like doves behind your veil;
Your hair is like a flock of goats
That have descended from Mount Gilead."

Okay, some cultural context here. Don't use the "hair like a flock of goats" line on your woman. Back in that day, it was a very hot thing to say to a woman. Today, it would obviously fall flat. Say something like, "I love your hair because it's so soft, smooth, and luxuriant." (For some great "hair lines," read her shampoo and conditioner bottles.)

Solomon (4:2)

"Your teeth are like a flock of newly shorn ewes
Which have come up from their washing,

All of which bear twins,

And not one among them has lost her young."

You've got to be kidding me! One whole verse dedicated to her teeth? In that day, it was a big deal for a woman to have all her teeth. Talk about details! I can relate, though. Sandy has a little space between her two front teeth. I love that space and tell her often that it's a part of her beauty.

Solomon doesn't stop at her teeth. Oh, no. He keeps going down her body, describing every beautiful part: her lips, mouth, and temples are next (4:3). Who cares about temples? He does. He wants her to know that he thinks she has magnificent temples. When was the last time you complimented your wife's temples? I thought so.

In 4:4, Solomon expands his praise to Shulamith's character:

"Your neck is like the tower of David

Built with rows of stones,

On which are hung a thousand shields,

All the round shields of the mighty men."

Solomon tells her that her neck is not only physically attractive, but it also reveals some wonderful internal qualities. She carries herself with strength, dignity, and integrity. He wants her to know she is beautiful physically and as a person. Shulamith, like every woman, yearns for her man to find her beautiful outside *and* for the beauty that is inside.

Finally, in 4:5:

"Your two breasts are like two fawns,

Twins of a gazelle."

What took so long? Solomon wants to make sure that she realizes that it isn't just about her breasts. They're part of the gorgeous package, but not the focus of his desire and love. Every single physical part and every single character quality is beautiful.

In case she's still wondering if he thinks she's beautiful, Solomon closes the deal in 4:7 with these powerful words:

"You are altogether beautiful, my darling,
And there is no blemish in you."

Oh, come on! Isn't this overkill? Everybody has flaws! That's right, everybody does have flaws. Everybody but your wife! That's what Solomon is saying to Shulamith. She is not only beautiful, inside and out. Her beauty is perfect to him. Period.

When I'm teaching a seminar on the Song of Solomon and reach chapter four, I tell the men: "Your wife is the most beautiful woman in the world. Right? Well, then, tell her. Do it now. Let's practice. When I raise my hand in a moment, I want every husband here to whisper in his wife's ear: 'You are the most beautiful woman in the world.' And, whisper one reason why that's true. It could be a physical feature, a character trait, or a spiritual quality. All right, go! And make her believe it."

The wives love this. Absolutely love it! Then, I add: "Is doing this once a year good enough? No! Every six months? No! Once every month? No! Husbands, tell her she's beautiful with a specific reason *every day*."

My great friend, Bob Johns, is a master at telling his wife, Pam, that she's beautiful. When Sandy and I are with the Johns, Bob will comment on Pam's beauty more than once. Pam loves it, and she loves Bob for doing it.

Bob and Solomon know you need to convince your wife every day that you think she is the most beautiful woman on the earth. When you get that done, how will she respond? The same way Shulamith responds to Solomon's praise in chapter four of the Song.

In 4:11–5:1, there is a very erotic description of exactly how Shulamith responds to Solomon and his heartfelt compliments about her beauty. They have deep intimate kisses (4:11), she is very sexually aroused (4:15), she urges him to come inside her (4:16), and they have intensely pleasurable intercourse (5:1).

Shulamith gives herself completely and passionately to Solomon. I think you get the picture.

"Come Over Here, You Stud"

Just a few verses later, Shulamith goes on her own rant of praise for Solomon. As Solomon did, she begins with a general statement of praise.

Shulamith (5:10)
"My beloved is dazzling and ruddy,
Outstanding among ten thousand."

She describes him as a strikingly attractive man. He's not just good looking. He's dazzling. But she also wants Solomon to know that she deeply respects his character. He is outstanding. He is extremely impressive to her.

Solomon, as every man does, yearns for his woman to think he's a physical stud and to be impressed with him as a person. Shulamith knows this truth and so continues to praise his physical attractiveness and excellent character.

Shulamith (5:12)
"His eyes are like doves . . ."

She loves his eyes because they are soft and express his love for her.

Shulamith (5:13a)
"His cheeks are like a bed of balsam . . ."

She adores his cheeks—the cheeks on his face, in case you were wondering. (I bet she likes his other cheeks too!)

Shulamith (5:13b)
"His lips are lilies,
Dripping with liquid myrrh."

She's crazy about his lips. His kisses are gentle and sweet.

Shulamith (5:14b)
"His abdomen is carved ivory . . ."

The man has abs of ivory! At least, she thinks so. She is also commenting on his strength.

Shulamith (5:15a)
"His legs are pillars of alabaster . . ."

She admires his powerful body and believes he is unshakable in times of trouble.

Shulamith (5:15b)
"His appearance is like Lebanon,
Choice as the cedars."

She tells him he is a distinguished, regal person who possesses great dignity.

At this point in a marriage seminar, I tell the wives it's their turn to take a few minutes and whisper some praise into their husbands' ears. I say, "Your husband is the most impressive man in the world. Right? Well, then, tell him. When I raise my hand, whisper into his ear, 'You are my man and you are outstanding.' And, whisper one reason why that's true. It could be a physical feature like his cheeks, a character trait, or a spiritual quality."

Although the husbands love it, the wives seem to love it even more. The ladies usually get carried away and keep on talking and touching their husbands.

In 5:16, Shulamith describes their mutual passionate response to her words of praise for Solomon:

"His mouth is full of sweetness,
And he is wholly desirable."

We know Solomon is responding to her, because of the "sweetness" in his mouth. This phrase refers to the tender and kind way he speaks to her. Only a lover speaks this way. And there's no question Shulamith wants him. She finds him very desirable.

Idealize Your Spouse

The Song teaches that you need to see your spouse as perfect. Not really, really great. Not terrific. Perfect. I think the passages I've already discussed make this point clear, but here are a few more.

Solomon (1:8)
   "Most beautiful among women"

Solomon (4:7)

"Altogether beautiful . . . no blemish in you"

Solomon (5:2)

"My perfect one"

Shulamith (1:16)

"Handsome, pleasant"

Solomon (6:9)

"My perfect one . . . pure . . . blessed"

This is not overkill. This is not over the top. It's how you need to view your precious spouse. That is, if you want passion.

Stop Being a Crab—Think Positive

Stop crabbing about your partner's faults and annoying habits. You are a whiner! Do you want to see a real pest with all kinds of weaknesses? Look in the mirror! Satan wants you to focus on the negative. He'll use your negativity to kill your love. He's done it to millions of couples, and he wants you to be next.

Focus instead on your partner's positives. If you're really mired in a negative mind-set, write down a few of your wife's good points on a three-by-five card and carry it around with you. Look at the card often, and think about those positives. Dwell on them. Pray that God will help you see and appreciate your spouse's positive qualities.

Give your partner, in person, one positive statement per day. It can be physical: "Your eyes are beautiful." "I find your feet attractive." "Look at those abs!" It could be a character trait: "You're kind." "You're patient." "You have integrity." "I love your sense of humor." It could be a spiritual quality: "You're a godly person." "You love Jesus." "I admire you for having regular quiet times." "Thank you for praying with me last night."

Also, twice a day tell your spouse in person, "I love you." These three words convey a powerful, positive message. Don't tell me you're not an expressive person or that you never heard your parents say these words to each other. Just do it.

Out with the Negative, In with the Positive

Negatives destroy passion. You know that, don't you? Let's say you and your spouse are in the bedroom preparing to make love and these are your thoughts:

Husband: "I wish she wasn't such a sheet hog! She slurps her soup like an animal. She's gained a few pounds."

Wife: "He's been late getting home from work three times this week. He hasn't unloaded the dishwasher in two weeks. He took that last piece of pie last night."

Boy, this is going to be a super sexual time, isn't it? When you dwell on your spouse's negatives, sex and every other area of your marriage is damaged.

When you dwell on your spouse's positives, three great things happen. One, it will stimulate *in you* feelings of closeness and passion for your spouse. Two, it will stimulate *in your spouse* feelings of closeness and passion for you. Three, it will result in passion.

I will add a fourth benefit: it will lead, inevitably, to great sex. And isn't that why you bought this book?

7

"We're Not Having Any Fun!"

A lot of women are professional shoppers. They love to shop. They live to shop. Most men think about sex once every seven seconds. Most women think about shopping once every five seconds. My Sandy is no exception. I've seen her in full shopping mode, and let me tell you, she is a force of nature. When she hits the mall, don't get in her way. You *will* get hurt.

For Sandy, shopping is a thrilling adventure with no time limits. She usually has an idea of what she wants, but is open to all possibilities. She'll see what happens. She enjoys the entire experience: planning the shopping trip, talking about what she's thinking of buying, the actual shopping trip, showing the kids and me what she purchased, trying on any clothes she purchased and giving a fashion show, and calling family members and girlfriends to describe in excruciating detail the items she purchased.

Of course, sometimes Sandy comes home empty-handed from a shopping safari. She can shop for three hours and buy nothing. Absolutely nothing! Amazingly, coming home with zilch doesn't bother her in the least! She considers it time well spent. She does love to buy things, but that's only a part of the adventure. She also loves looking at all the items, talking with all the salespersons, and spending time with her shopping companions.

When I'm shopping with Sandy and it looks as though she's not going to buy anything, I panic. I've told her, "Honey, please buy something! Anything! How about that antique Chinese vase? I don't care if it's five hundred dollars. Buy it. If you buy nothing, we've wasted our time!"

When I shop, if I'm not able to buy what I came to buy, it's a disaster! I'm furious. I feel cheated. Humiliated. I have lost. I've failed to achieve my objective. For me, a shopping trip is a mission. Operation: Locate and Buy Something I Need. I have a clearly defined item as my goal, tight time parameters, and I zero in on accomplishing the mission.

The differences between men and women in the shopping arena are huge. Let me illustrate with how Sandy and I each shop for shoes. (Before I describe the shoe-shopping process, it's important to note that Sandy has at least two dozen pairs of shoes.) I am the proud and cost conscious owner of three pairs of shoes. When one of my three pairs of shoes wears out, I go to the shoe store and buy the exact same pair of shoes. I walk in and tell the sales clerk I want to buy the same shoes I'm wearing. He hands me the shoebox. I buy the shoes. I walk back to my car, and I drive away. I'm thinking, "Wow! That took ten minutes. A new record! And

I beat that guy in the Florida Gator T-shirt to the counter. Sweet!"

When Sandy shops for shoes, it takes as much time and effort as the Lewis and Clark expedition across America. She goes to the mall and walks through twenty shoe stores. She touches eighty percent of the shoes in those stores and tries on fifty percent. She has a pretty good idea of the kind of shoe she wants, but is in no hurry to find it.

She wanders up and down the aisles of shoes, searching for that one perfect pair of shoes. It's out there. She knows it's out there. She picks up a pair, feels them, turns them around, talks about how she feels about them, and mentions the outfits she could wear with them. If a pair passes this initial inspection, she'll try it on and walk around. She asks me what I think—like it matters—and then replaces the shoes and moves on.

Sandy gets distracted continually by other stores and the items they offer for sale. She'll exclaim, "Oh, that's cute," and walk over to the cute item and finger it. I say, "I thought we were shopping for shoes." She gives me a look that says, "You don't get it, do you? I'm shopping here!" She ends up going into every store in the mall, with the exception of the tobacco shop.

Sandy's checklist for a pair of shoes is: style, color, brand, fit, outfits it will match, price, and friendliness of the salesperson. Speaking for myself, I don't care if Frankenstein is the salesperson, as long as he is holding the box with the shoes I want. But for her, the most important determining factor is her *vibe* about the shoes. How do they make her feel? No vibe, no purchase. Sandy will wait two hours or twenty hours until she gets the vibe. When that bolt of intuition and inspiration strikes, that's when she will buy the shoes.

No More Shopping, No More Fun

For the first eight to ten years of our marriage, I went regularly with Sandy on her shopping trips. That's why I can describe them so well. But frankly, I got tired of going with her. I began to have these kind of thoughts: "I hate shopping. The way she shops drives me nuts! She takes way too long. Do I care about women's shoes, women's clothes, fabric, pillowcases, and the million other things she loves to buy?"

So, I stopped going with Sandy on shopping trips. And it was a big mistake. I was focusing on the shopping and not on Sandy. I missed having these blocks of time with her. I missed having fun with her. I missed the funny little things she'd say and do while shopping. I missed goofing off, teasing, and playing around with her on these trips. I missed the opportunities for spontaneous, playful conversations with her. Plus, I stayed home with four kids and they drove me nuts!

I'm ashamed to admit it took me years to realize what I was missing. What *we* were missing. It's not just about the shopping! It's also about being with my most favorite person in the world, and the fun we create together!

So, I'm back to shopping with Sandy now. I don't go with her every time she shops. I'm not the most terrific husband. But I do go fairly often. I still hate to shop, but I love Sandy, and I love being with her. We have fun. We play. We connect. We get closer.

"I Don't Want to Do What You Want to Do"

Many couples make the same mistake Sandy and I made. After a few years of marriage, they stop engaging in activities they used to do together. If a spouse doesn't enjoy a particular activity, he/she stops doing it. Hey, isn't that the American way? If I don't want to do something, I don't have to do it.

> It used to be: "I don't care what we do, as long as we are together."
> Now, it's: "I don't want to go to the mall with you."
> "I don't want to watch the ballgame with you."
> "I don't like going to the beach."
> "I don't like your television shows."
> "I don't want to walk around the neighborhood with you."
> "I loathe bowling."
> "I can't stand golf."
> "I don't want to rollerblade with you."

You can see the selfishness, can't you? What happens is the two of you gradually pull apart. You lose opportunities for spontaneous, playful experiences together. You lead increasingly separate lives. You each do more activities on your own.

The lack of fun time together spreads to other areas of the relationship. Even when you could be together, you stay apart. In the evening, you are very often doing different activities in different rooms. Communication goes down. Romance goes down. Sex goes down. You're not having fun anymore.

Boring Each Other to Death

When you go out together on a "date," it's not romantic. It's not playful. It's not a time of fun and laughter. You're going through the motions. It's a good idea to go out on dates, so that's what you're doing. It's better than nothing, but not by much.

"We had a nice time," you say. A date is not supposed to be a "nice time." You have a "nice time" with your mother, or your Aunt Bertha. A real date with your spouse ought to be fun, stimulating, romantic, and sensual. That's why you got married!

When you go out to eat, it's not only about where you go and what you eat. It's also about your conversation and the resulting romance, intimacy, and sex. When you go to a movie, it's not only about the movie. It's also about being together, talking about the movie, and discussing how the movie relates to your personal lives and relationship. When you go to a concert or a play, is it about the specific performance? You know the answer. No! It's also about sharing the experience and developing conversations about what happens when you're together.

This is why I can go shopping with Sandy and have a great time. I enjoy what happens between us during the shopping trip. Even if you both enjoy the activity, the activity alone should never be the focus. The focus is the unpredictable fun, laughter, chemistry, intimacy, and sexual desire you create during the activity.

Stop with the Lame Excuses

Here are the top seven lame excuses married couples have given me to explain why they no longer do fun, playful activities together. I have included my brilliant therapeutic responses.

Lame Excuse #1: "We save fun activities for special occasions."

Dave Clarke: "Bad idea. There aren't enough special occasions each year to keep a romantic, playful spark in your marriage. Do you have sex only on special occasions? To get quality, you always need quantity. You need one fun activity per week."

Lame Excuse #2: "We can't afford to go out all the time. Money is tight."

Dave Clarke: "First, you can't afford not to. Second, going out can be cheap. Get creative with your activities. There are many things you can do for next to nothing. In fact, the cheap dates are usually the best ones."

Lame Excuse #3: "We have small kids at home."

Dave Clarke: "That's exactly why the two of you have to get out of there! Your kids are killing your romance and passion. That's why God created babysitters."

Lame Excuse #4: "We don't have any activities that we both enjoy."

Dave Clarke: "Yes, you do. You just haven't found them yet. Also, it isn't necessary for both to enjoy a particular activity. Being together and having fun interacting is what it's all about."

Lame Excuse #5: "We're too busy."

Dave Clarke: "You're breaking my heart. Sandy and I had four small kids at home and we went out together regularly. You always make time for what's important."

Lame Excuse #6: "We're not doing too well as a couple right now, so this isn't a good time to go out together."

Dave Clarke: "I know you're not doing well. That's why you're in a shrink's office. Because you're not doing well, now is the perfect time to go out and create some fun. If you wait until you feel like it, it'll never happen. Do the behaviors and the feelings will follow. Sure, you'll have to force yourselves to do it. So what? Change can occur through new behaviors."

Bedroom Blues

You begin a relationship with a member of the opposite sex because you are physically attracted to that person. The physical chemistry between you two is thick. You are mesmerized by the beauty of your partner. You can't keep your hands off each other.

During dating and for the first few years of marriage, your physical relationship remains strong and vibrant. You're like a couple of kids, laughing and playing with each other. You flirt. You tease. You talk about sex. You make out and enjoy intercourse often.

But then, your infatuation runs out. The kids come. Your jobs make more and more demands on your time and energy. The fun, the spontaneity, and the playfulness are squeezed out of your marriage. You're not joyful, exuberant lovers anymore.

You're Mom and Dad. You're Mr. and Mrs. Job. You're business partners. You're roommates. You're too busy. Too stressed. Way too serious. You're too wrapped up in life's hectic pace and responsibilities to have fun with each other. You're still physically attracted to each other, and you still have sex, but your level of passion is greatly reduced.

You don't talk and joke about sex. Making out is a dim memory. The only time you kiss and play is during intercourse. This, in itself, is a *huge* mistake and a sign of decreasing passion. You don't have intercourse as much as you used to, and when you do, it has all the passion and intensity of a business meeting. It's quiet. Civilized. Routine. Boring.

What happened to you? You've stopped playing with each other. Sex, at its heart, is play. If you're not playful *outside* the bedroom, you can't be playful *inside* the bedroom.

Reverse the Funectomy

Do you want your passion back? Do you want your feelings of joy and excitement back? Do you want your great sex back? I know you do.

What's the answer? I'm going to tell you what I tell all the married couples I see in therapy: "Be honest with each other. Without meaning to, you've performed a funectomy on your marriage. The fun is gone. It's time to bring the fun back, and I can tell you how to do it."

8

Make Your Marriage a Romantic Comedy

To create the right mood for this chapter, I will retell the ending of one of the world's best-loved romantic comedies. Over the years, this film's tender, funny, and magical message has touched the hearts of millions of lovers.

The final scene opens with the camera showing two persons at the edge of a cliff overlooking an ocean. The scenery is breathtaking. The sun is about to drop into the water at the horizon. The sky is painted with a kaleidoscope of stunning colors. The perfect romantic setting.

The camera zooms in and we see that the two persons are none other than the hero and heroine of the movie. They are old now. Quite old. The man is in a wheelchair with a blanket covering his withered legs. His faithful wife stands behind him, her hands resting on the wheelchair handles. Their last dialogue begins:

> Wife: "Well, this is where it all ends after sixty-five years of marriage. I've been yearning for and dreading this moment for most of our married life."
>
> Husband: "What do you mean, ends? I'm in pretty bad shape, but I'm not dead yet."
>
> Wife: "You're very close to death. Closer than you think."
>
> Husband: "What? Do you know something I don't? And what do you mean by 'yearning for and dreading this moment'?"
>
> Wife: "I've yearned for years to tell you what I really think about you and our marriage. I dread the possibility of going to prison for the rest of my life."
>
> Husband: "Prison? Why would you go to prison?"
>
> Wife: "Because, after I've said what I want to say, I'm going to push you over the edge of this cliff. I'll keep the wheelchair and sell it for a few bucks. Now, be quiet and listen. When I married you, I dreamed of having a wonderful marriage. I wanted laughter, fun, and passion. I wanted excitement, spontaneity, and sensuality. What I got for most of those sixty-five years was a boring, ho-hum, and passionless marriage. You could say I'm a little bitter. So, this is goodbye."

As the camera pulls back, the old woman begins to rock her husband's wheelchair back and forth at the edge of the cliff. His pleas for mercy mingle with her high-pitched, cackling laugh as the screen fades to black. We're left to wonder if she actually dumped him over the edge.

Well, I guess you've figured out no one's ever made a romantic comedy with this story line. I don't think it would sell too many tickets. However, it has been my experience that many married couples end up just like this one. Not at the edge of a cliff with murder in mind. But with a mediocre, blah marriage that never realized its potential for passion.

If you want to avoid this metaphorical cliff in your marriage, you must learn how to inject frequent, liberal doses of fun and playfulness into your relationship. Who can teach you? Solomon and Shulamith.

Let's Play

Solomon and Shulamith are two of the original daters. They love to go out together. And, boy, do they know how to have fun! And the fun they have stokes their passion.

Shulamith (2:10)
"My beloved responded and said to me,
Arise, my darling, my beautiful one,
And come along."

Solomon asks Shulamith to leave home and come with him on a date. Take note, husbands: calling your wife "darling" and "beautiful one" increases the chances she'll want to go out with you.

In 2:11–13, Solomon shares his excitement about being with Shulamith on their outing:

For behold, the winter is past,
The rain is over and gone.
The flowers have already appeared in the land;
The time has arrived for pruning the vines,
And the voice of the turtledove
has been heard in our land.

> The fig tree has ripened its figs,
>> And the vines in blossom
>> have given forth their fragrance.
>> Arise, my darling, my beautiful one,
>> And come along!

He compares their love to the coming of spring. It is fresh, new, and beautiful. He wants to go out into this new world and enjoy it with her. He can't wait to spend time with her.

Solomon (2:14)
> "O my dove, in the clefts of the rock,
>
> In the secret place of the steep pathway,
>
> Let me see your form,
>
> Let me hear your voice;
>
> For your voice is sweet,
>
> And your form is lovely."

Why is Solomon asking Shulamith out? To have fun with her, to get to know her better as a person, *and* eventually to see her beautiful body.

Shulamith is not a passive, demure, little lady. Oh, no! She is attracted to Solomon and makes no bones about the fact that she wants to be with him sexually. Check out her erotic proposal to Solomon:

Shulamith (7:11)
> "Come, my beloved, let us go out into the country,
>
> Let us spend the night in the villages."

She asks Solomon to explore the countryside and, later that night, to explore her body. She wants sex! She doesn't have to ask him twice.

Shulamith (7:12)

> "Let us rise early and go to the vineyards;
> Let us see whether the vine has budded
> And its blossoms have opened,
> And whether the pomegranates have bloomed.
> There I will give you my love."

One date followed by intercourse isn't enough for Shulamith. This is a two-day date. It's a getaway. She wants to play with Solomon in the vineyards and then make love outside!

Solomon and Shulamith love being alone. It's not what they do that's important. What excites them is just being in each other's company. The same progression is evident in both these passages: going out together, being playful and having fun, and capping it off with passionate sex.

Get Out of the Home

It's important to go out regularly on fun, playful dates. Shoot for once a week. At the bare minimum, go out once every two weeks. No kids. No pets. No family. No friends. Just the two of you.

Don't do the same old, boring routine of dinner and a movie. You have two brains. Use them! Be creative! Do activities you did back when you were dating. These will bring back great memories and romantic feelings.

You are going out to play. Do what your partner enjoys. Find an activity that you both enjoy. If necessary, alternate the activities on your dates.

Mall	Picnic in a Park
Trade Show	Frisbee
Car Show	Tennis

Craft Fair	Bowling
Beach	Golf
Garage Sale-ing	Dancing

The list of possible activities is almost endless. Look for activities that allow you to interact and communicate. Again, it's not what you do that is the key. It's being together and having fun.

Another idea is to play practical jokes on your friends. Sandy is a master of this genre. One time several years ago, we toilet-papered the home of Wayne and Denise Hall. They were inside and didn't have a clue. Sandy and I wore black clothes and pulled off the commando mission with skill and flair. And a lot of laughter. The best part was leaving a note implicating my best friend, Rocky Glisson, as the culprit. It was sweet and a total riot to nail both the Halls and Rocky with one prank!

Have Fun in the Home

Loosen up in your home and look for ways to be playful. Silly comments. Good-natured teasing. Crazy board games. Funny little notes left for your spouse. Point out stories in the newspaper about people who do incredibly dumb things. Think goofy and immature, and you'll be on the right track.

I love being playful with Sandy in the home. She loves it too. One time, I was home at lunchtime on a weekday. It looked like rain, so I told Sandy I was leaving early to get to work to beat the rain. It was dark, windy, and you could hear the rumbling of thunder.

I walked up to Sandy, took her in my arms, and said, "Baby, it's going to start pouring any second. But do I care?

No. I want—no, I need—one more stolen kiss before I go. This kiss may cost me. I may get soaked, but it's worth it to taste your ruby red lips." And I parked a real smoocher on her.

Dumb? Sure. Silly? Certainly. Fun and playful? Oh, yeah.

Another time, Sandy and I were watching a television sitcom with two of our kids. In the show, a guy had expressed romantic interest in a female coworker, and she had turned him down.

After the show ended, Sandy went into the kitchen. I followed her, took her in my arms, kissed her, and said in a loud voice so the kids could hear: "When you expressed interest in me back in college, twenty-eight years ago, what did I do? I guess it's pretty obvious what I did! And twenty-five years of marriage and four kids later, I'm so glad I did. I would do it again. I love you!"

Sandy laughed and then gave me a big, lip-smacking kiss. The kids made gagging sounds, but we didn't care. It was a moment of playfulness. Solomon and Shulamith would be proud of us.

Terms of Endearment

"I love you, Sweetie Carkst." This is one of my many special names for Sandy, and I call her this often. "Sweetie Carkst?" you ask. Carkst is a form of Clarke. Well, it's hard to explain. All I can tell you is that my calling Sandy a variety of pet names—and vice versa—is a good practice. It's biblical, and Sandy and I like it.

Solomon and Shulamith use pet names for each other throughout the Song. It's part of their playfulness. Take a look.

Solomon calls Shulamith "my darling" in:

1:9	4:1
1:15	4:7
2:2	5:2
2:10	6:4
2:13	

Shulamith calls Solomon "my beloved" in:

1:13	5:5
1:14	5:6
1:16	5:8
2:3	5:10
2:8	5:16
2:9	6:2
2:10	6:3
2:16	7:9
2:17	7:10
4:16	7:11
5:2	7:13
5:4	8:14

Solomon also calls Shulamith "my dove" (2:14; 5:2; 6:9), "my bride" (4:8, 9, 10, 11, 12; 5:1), and "my perfect one" (5:2; 6:9).

My personal favorites are names Shulamith calls Solomon three times: "gazelle" or "young stag" (2:9, 17; 8:14). In today's language, this means "stud" or "hunk." Now, what husband wouldn't love to hear this as a pet name?

So, "darlings" and "beloveds": don't stop using pet names for each other. Be gushy. Be mushy. Be sentimental. Be syrupy sweet. Be lovey-dovey. As Solomon and Shulamith demonstrate, those special endearments add playfulness and a romantic spark to a love relationship.

You Are Such a Flirt!

The lost art of marital flirting is in full, shameless display in the Song. Solomon flirts. You kind of expect that from the guy. But Shulamith is just as big a flirt. And that doesn't make her a bad girl. Hardly. That makes her a girl madly in love.

Solomon and Shulamith, with the full blessing and approval of God, make all kinds of sexually suggestive comments to each other. They tease. They joke about sex. They describe each other's bodies in vivid detail. They talk about making love. They talk about various sexual positions. It is not inappropriate. It is not nasty. It is beautiful.

You might want to take a cold shower before you read the following verses. On second thought, forget the cold shower. Let these verses arouse your sexual passion for your spouse.

Shulamith (1:2)

"May he kiss me with the kisses of his mouth!
For your love is better than wine."

Right at the beginning of the book, Shulamith is doing some serious flirting. She's begging Solomon to kiss her! This kind of talk is beyond erotic for a man.

Shulamith (1:4)

"Draw me after you and let us run together!
The king has brought me into his chambers."

In case he didn't get the message the first time, she asks Solomon to take her into his bedroom and make love to her.

Shulamith (1:16)

"How handsome you are, my beloved,
And so pleasant!
Indeed, our couch is luxuriant!"

She is not talking about the furniture here. She is referring to their being in bed together. And what do lovers do in bed?

Shulamith (2:6)

"Let his left hand be under my head
And his right hand embrace me."

She describes an extremely intimate position: the embrace of two lovers.

Shulamith (8:2–3)

"I would lead you and bring you
Into the house of my mother, who used to instruct me;
I would give you spiced wine to drink from the juice of
my pomegranates.
Let his left hand be under my head,
And his right hand embrace me."

Shulamith gives Solomon an erotic proposal. She offers him her body and asks him to drink in her sensual delights.

Solomon (2:14b)

"Let me see your form,
Let me hear your voice;
For your voice is sweet,
And your form is lovely."

As we've seen before in looking at this verse, Solomon is praising her physical beauty. He is looking forward to seeing her naked.

Solomon (4:9)

"You have made my heart beat faster, my sister, my bride;

You have made my heart beat faster with a single glance of your eyes,

With a single strand of your necklace."

Solomon tells her, twice, that she sexually excites him like no other woman. She is an absolute babe, and he wants her to know it.

In 4:12–14, Solomon describes in exquiste detail Shulamith's beautiful body and their lovemaking. He uses the image of a garden. A "garden" filled with all kinds of sexual delights. Then, he really gets personal.

Solomon (4:15)

"You are a garden spring,

A well of fresh water,

And streams flowing from Lebanon."

Whoa! This is beyond personal. He's telling Shulamith that she is sexually aroused and prepared for intercourse. No way! Is this in the Bible? Yes!

Solomon (5:1)

"I have come into my garden, my sister, my bride;

I have gathered my myrrh along with my balsam.

I have eaten my honeycomb and my honey;

I have drunk my wine and my milk . . ."

Here, Solomon delicately describes their intercourse with the illustration of a feast. Gutsy. And very erotic. When was the last time you had intercourse, and then described to your spouse what happened?

God is not upset in the least with all this sexual frivolity. He is delighted with their sexual play. That's why all this flirting and sexual talk is in the Song. Between a husband and a wife, it is not just okay to do it. It's great to do it.

Dust Off Your Flirting Skills

Okay, it's time for you two to get back in the flirting saddle. Start flirting with each other verbally. Start talking in a sensual, romantic, and sexual way. Be spicy! Be a little outrageous. Let your hair down. Let your belt out a notch or two. Make sexual, flirty comments in person, on the phone, by email, in texts, in handwritten notes, and with soap on your bathroom mirror.

> "You look hot in that top, baby!"
> "I'm looking forward to tonight, stud!"
> "You are one sexy chick!"
> "I want you, I need you, I have to have you!"

I could go on, but I think you get the idea. Unless you had an arranged marriage, you used to flirt with each other. Flirting is what lovers do. So do it.

Deep down, no man wants a prim, tidy, proper, and straight-laced woman. He wants a flirty, sensuous woman who comes on to him. Deep down, no woman wants an inhibited, prudish, buttoned-down, stick of a man. She wants a man who isn't afraid to share his romantic and sexual feelings with her. She wants a stud muffin.

The Original and Best

The Song of Solomon is the original romantic comedy. Because God is the Creative Producer and Director, it's the best. Solomon and Shulamith show us that to be crazy in love, you must be playful. You have to have fun. You have to act like a couple of kids!

Love is the *greatest*, and nothing could be more serious. But the physical and emotional expression of love between lovers is *not* serious. Love is fun. Love is a blast.

Some of you are thinking: "Boy, Dave, I don't know if I can pull off this kind of playfulness."

You say: "That's not me. I wasn't raised that way."

God says: "I know, but try it my way."

You say: "That's not my style. I'm too conservative. I can't let myself go like that."

God says: "I know you are this way, but try it my way."

In the Song of Solomon, God is saying: "Here's how to keep your love fresh and exciting. It worked three thousand years ago, and it will work for you now."

9 ·

"We Can't Kiss Anymore"

Do you want to know if you've lost the romance in your marriage? I have a very simple, foolproof test that will provide the answer. I call it "The Kissing Test." In my twenty plus years as a psychologist in private practice and a marriage seminar leader, I've never once had this test fail to detect the absence of romance in a marriage.

Here's how the test works. If, on a regular basis, you and your spouse are kissing in one of the four following ways, you have lost your romance for each other. And if you've lost your romance, you've lost your passion.

Ready? All right, let's go.

The Pathetic Little Peck Kiss

A husband and a wife are living in the same house, apartment, or condo. They're in love. At least, they're supposed to be in love. They once were in love. It's a weekday morning, and they are getting ready to go their separate ways. The good news is, they're going to kiss. The bad news is, here's how they're going to do it.

They come together and, standing fairly close, they each say, "Goodbye, honey. Have nice day." Then, the climactic moment comes, and their two sets of absolutely bone dry lips touch for a millisecond. Or, a nanosecond. Whichever is the briefer.

They have successfully completed the classic "Pathetic Little Peck Kiss." It's really more of a bump than a kiss. The lips are thinned out and hard. A couple of nubs, barely touching. It's about as exciting as exchanging business cards. No moisture. No fun. No joy. Above all, no passion.

The "Peck" is the kind of kiss you give to your Aunt Sarah, your mother, or your great-grandmother. It's polite. It's appropriate. It's civilized. Genteel, even. But is the Peck any way to kiss your sweetheart? Your lover? The most wonderful person in the world? Your mate for life? No! It's not. And, deep down, you know it.

The sad, truly embarrassing story of the Peck isn't quite over. This husband and wife go through the day with a longing in their hearts. They love each other so much and miss each other so much . . . that when they see each other again, they follow the same old Peck routine. "Hi, honey, how was your day? Pretty good? Yeah, me too. Come over here." And the same, dry as dust, nubbed-out lips touch ever so quickly.

Is this any way to express love? Is this any way to begin an evening of romance and passion? Of course not.

The Poofy Lip Kiss

To perform the "Poofy Lip Kiss," the second type of kissing, the husband and wife stand a few feet away from each other.

This is kissing while standing as far apart as possible. Not a good start, is it? Then, they lean forward from the waist. They don't want to wrinkle their clothes! They don't want to smear the lady's makeup! They don't want any other body parts touching! They have enough children, thank you.

As they lean, they push their necks out as far as possible, and their hands go up in a Barney the Dinosaur, I-have-to-protect-myself kind of way. Their lips are *poofed* out or bunched and barely graze as the kiss is completed.

The Sound Effect Kiss

In this third, ridiculous, waste-of-time attempt at a kiss, the man and woman are at home, and one spouse is leaving for a while. He—or she—is going to work, running an errand, taking the kids to school, going jogging. . . . The man and woman are standing twenty—maybe even twenty-five—feet apart. It is a huge, gaping chasm that they can't hope to cross.

The leaving spouse turns, and, after saying, "Goodbye, honey," or, "See you later," puckers up and makes the *sound* of a kiss. Is this a real kiss? No! It's just noise! The spouse being left makes some kind of a goodbye statement and sends a kissing *sound* back.

What's going on here? If this sounds like you, are the two of you acting out some kind of a radio drama? If you are, then you could have some fun and make the sounds of a door opening and closing and a car engine starting. But, instead of a radio drama, you are in real life. You're saying goodbye to the love of your life! And, when you do that, a real honest-to-goodness kiss is required.

Do you know what I say? You're only twenty, twenty-five feet apart! Why don't you just walk over to each other and put a significant, genuine kiss on each other's lips? I'll tell you why. Because you've lost the ability to kiss.

The Dreaded Kiss on the Cheek

I hesitate to even put down on paper this final, and most miserable, mistake of a kiss. I'll have to hold my nose while writing, but it must be done. Someone has to save you from yourselves.

I'll make this brief. You walk up to your dear spouse, lean in and pucker up for a kiss. Of course, you're assuming you'll be kissing on the lips because that's how most of the civilized world defines a kiss. You are sadly, tragically mistaken.

As you reach the point of impact, your lover and precious partner suddenly turns and offers you a cheek. A cheek! How impersonal! How insensitive! How rude! Lips to lips has a chance of generating some romance and a stirring of emotions. Lips to cheek is barely above a handshake on the scale of affection. If you are outraged—or, at least, deeply disappointed—at being forced to kiss your spouse's cheek, you're not that far gone. But if either of you is okay with cheek kissing, you are not in good romantic shape. You need help. That's where I come in.

You Are Romance Challenged

If you are guilty of regularly engaging in one or more of these kisses, you have almost certainly kissed romance goodbye. While "The Kissing Test" is a very accurate diagnostic tool, there are three other central mistakes made by romance-challenged couples. See if you can spot these mistakes in the following description of one week in the life of an unromantic couple.

Bob and Betty's Week of No Romance

It's Monday morning, and the alarm goes off. Another week has begun. Bob and Betty roll out of bed and mumble "Morning" to each other. They go through their usual weekday morning routine: individual devotions, wake up the kids, grab some breakfast, and go their separate ways. They engage in a lightning quick Peck of a kiss just before parting.

During the day, they have a few brief phone calls. Only routine, mundane matters are discussed: how their days are going, don't forget to pick up Susie from school, please get milk and bread from the store, and I think I'm developing a cold sore.

The evening goes pretty much like all their evenings. Helping the kids with homework, having dinner, playing with the kids, some time on the phone and computer, and the kids going to bed. Bob watching television and Betty reading a novel and having a few phone conversations with friends. They have a five-minute dialogue in the kitchen about needed home repairs and a school event coming up in four days.

At the end of the evening, they watch the news on television. Even though they are sitting together on the couch, there is no touching. They briefly discuss one of the news stories. After they get in bed, Bob kisses Betty on her cheek, and they both mumble, "Good night."

The next few days are exact copies of this day. Bob and Betty's morning, daytime, and evening routines remain the same. Bob watches some television shows that feature scantily clad women and steamy sex scenes. He knows it's wrong, but he's drawn to these shows because of the feeling they give him. He's also spending more time secretly staring at certain attractive women at work. He is talking more with one of these women. Of course, they are "just good friends," he tells himself.

Betty loses herself in her romance novels. She enjoys the fictional stories of men and women falling in love and doing all kinds of romantic things together. These stories stir her heart and make her feel more alive. She longs for this kind of heart-thumping, romantic feeling with Bob. But those days are over. He's just not that kind of guy. Plus, she has come to accept that romantic pursuit and passion are just not part of a real-life marriage.

On Friday night, both the kids have sleepovers at the homes of friends. Do Bob and Betty use the extra time and freedom to go out on a romantic date? No. Do they have a candlelight dinner at home? No. Do they engage in some serious kissing? No. Do they watch a romantic movie together at home? No. Do they at least seize this sudden golden opportunity to make love? Yes, they do. But, it's more "make sex" than "make love."

Even though they have plenty of time, Bob and Betty stick to their tried-and-true, it's-worked-for-years foreplay and intercourse routine. They kiss and touch the same way they always do. It's not about expressing love and feeling passion.

On Saturday night, they go out on one of their infrequent dates. They follow their usual pattern of dinner and a movie. During the evening, Bob ogles several women wearing cleavage-revealing outfits. Betty notices what he's doing, but says nothing. She fantasizes about the hero in the movie and wonders what it would be like being in a relationship with such a dashing, handsome man.

Sunday comes and goes without any romantic sparks. In church, Betty and Bob talk with two couples they've known for years. Betty admires both husbands and imagines what it would be like to be married to men who are obviously more romantic and affectionate than Bob. Bob checks out three or four women he finds attractive and wonders what it would be like to be with them sexually.

No Romance, No Passion, Big Trouble

Not a pretty story, is it? The really sad part is that it is a very common story. Millions of married couples are living almost exactly this way every week. Just as Bob and Betty do, they live without romance. Which means they live without passion. Which means they are not enjoying the marriage God wants them to enjoy.

Did you spot the three, central romantic mistakes in Bob and Betty's story? Mistake number one is the lack of romantic behaviors. Bob and Betty miss opportunity after opportunity to be romantic. They fail repeatedly to create romantic situations in the home and outside the home. They're not playful, that's for sure. Even when their kids are asleep or out of the home, they blow it!

Mistake number two is that they compared one another to others. If you think anyone else is superior to your spouse, you are killing your romance. Bob, as many husbands do, is fantasizing about the bodies of other women. Betty, as many women do, is fantasizing about the character traits and romantic qualities of other men. This is a very dangerous game. In addition to annihilating your romantic feelings for your mate, this kind of comparison is setting you up for an affair.

The third mistake is the absence of passionate, erotic kissing. Bob and Betty kiss only in a serious, sensual way during foreplay. And that is only once—at the most—during the week!

That's not enough kissing! Frequent and heartfelt kissing, in addition to just before intercourse, is essential to maintain a steady flow of romantic feelings. Bob and Betty don't know this, and it's taking a huge toll on the romance in their marriage.

Save Your Excuses and Get to Work

I ask just about every couple I see in therapy: "Why don't you create romantic situations and kiss as though you mean it?" I've heard every conceivable excuse for not engaging in these emotionally and physically romantic behaviors. Here's a brief sampling.

"I'm stressed."

"I've got to meet the needs of my kids."

"Why kiss her passionately if we can't have intercourse right away?"

"If we kiss passionately, he will want intercourse."

"I'm busy at work."

"I'm too tired."

"I have to get all the household chores done."

"I don't think she's interested."

"I don't think he's interested."

"I have a lot of resentments against my spouse."

"My back is sore."

"You haven't smelled my spouse's breath."

"We've already had our kids."

"Passion is for younger couples. We're old now and don't need it."

I always give the same thoughtful, compassionate, therapeutically appropriate response to all these excuses: "Baloney!"

Of course, that's not all I say. I continue with these words of truth and, hopefully, motivation: "God made the heart of every married person to be romantic, and to feel the passion that springs out of romance. He designed your hearts to need a regular cycle of romance and passion. Living without this cycle is death to your marriage and will put you both at great risk for an affair. So, let's get to work on your romance."

10 ·····································

"I Want to Be Kissed Passionately!"

Look, I have to be honest. There are some verses in the Song of Solomon that don't quite fit the theme of romance I'm developing in these chapters. I've written these troubling verses below. Read them, and then I'll try to explain what they mean.

> Solomon: "Although I do find you alluring, I confess I find myself drawn to other, more beautiful maidens."
>
> Shulamith: "You are indeed handsome, but you do not share words as sweet as a young man I know in the village."
>
> Solomon: "Our love is comfortable, like the well-worn tapestries in our bed chambers."

Shulamith: "Your kisses and tender caresses are not needed for me to feel close to your heart."

I'm sure you've figured out that you won't find these words anywhere in the Song. No way! Solomon and Shulamith never speak to each other in this way. They would pity any couple who does. By studying their words and their behavior, we can learn how to create and maintain an intense, sizzling romance in our marriages.

"You Are So Hot, Baby!"

The very first recorded words Solomon speaks to Shulamith, in chapter one of the Song, are some of the most romantic words in the entire book:

Solomon (1:9–10)
"To me, my darling, you are like
My mare among the chariots of Pharaoh.
Your cheeks are lovely with ornaments,
Your neck with strings of beads."

Why are these words so romantic? Because they come in response to Shulamith's comments about her physical appearance:

Shulamith (1:6)
"Do not stare at me because I am swarthy,
For the sun has burned me.
My mother's sons were angry with me;
They made me caretaker of the vineyards
But I have not taken care of my own vineyard."

Shulamith's dirtball brothers forced her to work outside, and the sun had turned her skin dark. In that day, fair skin was the standard of beauty. The other women were looking down on her because of her dark complexion. Even though she seems to be dealing confidently with this social rejection, it is significant that she mentions it.

In 1:9–10, Solomon immediately and powerfully assures her that he finds her extremely attractive physically. She is as beautiful as his horse. I wouldn't compare your wife to a horse if I were you, but back then this was a high compliment.

Solomon's language here indicates he desires to make love to her. Knowing she'd appreciate hearing some specific reasons why he sees her as beautiful, Solomon compliments her cheeks and her neck.

Just about every wife is insecure at times about her looks. She compares herself to other women—friends, strangers, women in the media—and feels inferior. Your job, husband, is to make her understand that to you, she is beautiful.

Solomon wants Shulamith to know that he thinks she is gorgeous. In case she harbors any doubts, he closes the deal with these words near the end of chapter one:

Solomon (1:15)
"How beautiful you are, my darling,
How beautiful you are!"

Why say it once when you can say it twice? The point here, for you, is: tell your wife often she is *physically* beautiful. That's what Solomon does throughout the Song. Read his words:

(2:10) "my beautiful one"
(2:13) "my beautiful one"
(4:1)   "How beautiful you are . . . How beautiful you are!"

(4:7)   "You are altogether beautiful"
(6:4)   "You are . . . beautiful . . . lovely . . . awesome"
(6:10) "beautiful"
(7:6)   "How beautiful . . . you are"

Solomon passes along a secret: When a woman is complimented on her physical beauty, she feels loved and confident and will respond with physical passion. She will think, "If you think my body is beautiful, I want you to touch it. I want to share it with you."

Yes, you notice other women. You're a man. But immediately get your eyes away from other women and back on your woman. And think to yourself: "That woman is attractive, but my woman is much more beautiful."

Husband, tell your wife often that she is beautiful. Never use the word "pretty." Your woman is beautiful. I disagree with writers who say it's okay to comment on another woman's beauty in front of your wife. How stupid is that? That hurts your wife and erodes her confidence in your opinion of her looks.

Although she doesn't do it as much, Shulamith also lets Solomon know she finds him very good-looking:

(1:16) "How handsome you are"
(5:10) "dazzling and ruddy"

We've already seen how, in 5:10–15, Shulamith goes into detail describing the beautiful parts of Solomon's body. So, wife, make it a regular practice to let your man know he is a physically striking stud.

Complimenting your spouse's physical beauty creates a romantic spark, produces a physically passionate response, and protects you from the dangers of focusing on the beauty of others.

Let's Get Romantic

Solomon and Shulamith were masters at creating romantic situations. They knew how to put themselves in a romantic mood in which they could experience feelings of love, intimacy, and intense pleasure.

Probably the best example in the Song of how the two lovers choreographed a series of romantic steps is 2:10–14. We've already seen (in chapter eight) how these verses display the playfulness of Solomon and Shulamith. But they also reveal some serious romance. The progression in this passage is: playfulness (2:10), followed by a romantic mood (2:11–13), and finally, a deep romantic interaction (2:14).

Solomon playfully asks Shulamith to go out with him into the great outdoors. He weaves a romantic mood, using vivid descriptions of the beauty of spring. Finally, he and Shulamith end up in a very private, very romantic setting:

Solomon (2:14)
"O my dove, in the clefts of the rock,
In the secret place of the steep pathway,
Let me see your form,
Let me hear your voice;
For your voice is sweet,
And your form is lovely."

They are alone. The entire world is shut out. They are connecting on a deep, emotional level. They are feeling physical chemistry and passion. It just doesn't get any more romantic than this.

Here is a list of behaviors that can help you and your lover create romantic situations:

Hold hands when you walk together.

Open your woman's car door for her.

Open the door of every building for your woman.

Walk your neighborhood holding hands.

Walk on the beach at sunset holding hands.

Walk by any body of water holding hands.

Go on a weekend getaway at a bed and breakfast.

Write each other love cards and notes.

Look through your wedding album together.

Watch a romantic movie at home.

Farm the kids out at a sleepover, and spend two hours making love.

Slow dance at home.

Have a candlelight dinner at home.

Use candles during your couple talk times.

I think you get the idea. Be playful, because that begins the process of romance. But also be intentionally romantic. Engage in specific behaviors that will lead to the romantic mood and feeling you want to enjoy.

Real Kissing

Any discussion of romance is incomplete without the subject of kissing. Kissing is incredibly romantic. That is, as long as you are kissing the correct way. In chapter nine, I've covered the four main kissing mistakes made by too many married couples. Now, it's time to cover the right way to kiss.

It should come as no surprise that Solomon and Shulamith are excellent kissers. World-class. The second verse in the Song is a kissing verse!

Shulamith (1:2)

"May he kiss me with the kisses of his mouth!"

Shulamith wants to be kissed! She's a pretty assertive chick. Do you think for a moment that she is asking for a Pathetic Little Peck, a Poofy Lip, a Sound Effect, or a Cheek kiss? Of course not! She wants a passionate kiss from her man, Solomon. She wants him to kiss her as though he means it.

Solomon doesn't need much encouragement to kiss Shulamith. He wants to kiss her!

Solomon (4:3)

"Your lips are like a scarlet thread,
And your mouth is lovely."

He's crazy about her lips and her mouth. He can't wait to kiss her. And that's exactly what he does, recorded just a few verses later:

Solomon (4:10)

"How beautiful is your love, my sister, my bride!
How much better is your love than wine . . ."

The two lovers begin to kiss, and Solomon raves that Shulamith tastes better than wine. To be able to make this comparison, he had to lay an industrial strength kiss or two on her ruby red lips.

All the kisses described in the Song are good, solid, put-your-heart-and-soul-into-it efforts. When Solomon and Shulamith kiss, they really kiss. They are expressing their love for each other. Each kiss communicates, "I'm crazy about you, sweetheart."

Read this next verse and see if you can identify the type of kiss it describes:

Solomon (4:11)
    "Your lips, my bride, drip honey;
    Honey and milk are under your tongue . . ."

French kissing! Right here in the Bible! Most commentators skip this verse or write that the milk and honey refer to the produce of the land. Oh, please! That's absurd! These commentators have forgotten how to kiss. The only way Solomon knows what her tongue tastes like is because he has used his tongue to find out. These lines portray kissing that becomes more and more intimate as it moves from lips to the tongue.

Shulamith (5:13b)
    "His lips are lilies dripping with liquid myrrh."

Are your kisses "dripping with liquid myrrh"? If not, you'd better get to work. Shulamith loves the taste and power of his wet kisses. Solomon's bride is also saying in this sensual picture that his breath is sweet.

Solomon (7:8b–9a)
    "And the fragrance of your breath like apples,
    And your mouth like the best wine!"

Solomon finds Shulamith's kisses absolutely delicious and very stimulating. Her breath is like apples, and her mouth tastes like the finest wine.

Shulamith (7:9b)

"It goes down smoothly for my beloved,
Flowing gently through the lips of those who fall asleep."

Shulamith describes their kisses as wine flowing smoothly through their lips. These are gentle but obviously passionate kisses. As their last kisses end, they fall asleep in each other's arms.

A Crash Course in Kissing

When you kiss, take your lover in your arms. A full-body, all-the-right-parts-touching, sensual hug is part of a great kiss. Put your arms around your lover, and then touch his/her beautiful face as you move in with your red-hot lips. Give your sweetheart a real kiss. A full-bore, involved, heartfelt smacker. A gum-scorching lip-lock. A kiss with a punch in it.

So many spouses pull back so fast from a kiss that they run the risk of whiplash. The idea is, you don't want to leave the luscious lips of your precious partner. Make your kiss last at least twenty seconds. Now that kind of kiss makes a statement! Instead of "How are you," you're saying, "I'm crazy about you!"

Is one kiss, even if it's a whopper, going to be enough? Of course not! How can you possibly stand to kiss your lover only one time? It's impossible! Or, it ought to be! Give multiple kisses. Two or three lingering smooches are a must.

You protest, "But Dave, how can I kiss like this when I'm rushing out the door to work?" First, it'll take you only about one minute. Second, why not leave feeling sexually excited? Is that a crime? I say it's a crime *not* to feel that way when you leave your lover. That jolt of sensual pleasure and attraction is a great way to start the day.

Kissing each other as though you mean it immediately produces a romantic connection. The more you give the kind of kisses I've described, the more romance you'll build in your relationship. So, kiss often! Kiss when you first wake up. Kiss when you part ways in the morning. Kiss when you see each other at the end of the workday. Kiss as part of your couple talk time in the evening. Kiss in the kitchen when you're getting a drink or snack. Kiss when you go to bed.

Kiss every time you leave each other, even if one of you is going to the bathroom. I tell Sandy, "Honey, I've got to go to the bathroom. These things happen. I'm sorry to leave you this way. Parting is such sweet sorrow. Remember me." And then I put a couple of real kisses on her sensuous mouth. She laughs, but she loves it.

Husband, the next time you leave your woman, lay a heart-thumping and teeth-rattling kiss on her fabulous lips. Pull back and say, "There's more where that came from, baby!" She'll be shocked. She'll be thrilled. She'll get the distinct impression that you love her and want her body.

The truth is, you don't need this course on kissing. It's more of a reminder than a how-to manual. You know how to kiss, don't you? You used to do it all the time. Remember those days? You didn't need anyone to teach you how to kiss in a passionate way. You did it naturally because you were in love. And, you practiced a lot.

Dust off your kissing skills and get back in the game! You have your instructions for romance, straight from two lovers who know all the ins and outs of romance. Follow Solomon and Shulamith's example and you will experience exhilarating romance that never ends.

11

"I'm Married to a Secret Agent!"

Communication presents a critical problem in most marriages. Why? Because The Talking Woman marries The Secret Agent Man.

The Talking Woman always has something to say. She expresses her thoughts. She expresses her feelings. She expresses her thoughts about her feelings. She expresses her feelings about her thoughts. She expresses her feelings about thoughts she hasn't even had yet.

Every event of her day has special meaning, is remembered, and is shared with more than one person. This morning she was flossing her teeth, and the floss shredded. As she looked at the two pieces of floss, she had a burst of happiness because they reminded her of the time she was water skiing at age thirteen and her ski rope broke. Even though that was a bummer, that day at the lake with her dad and Aunt Betty was great.

At four in the afternoon that day, she and Aunt Betty had a real heart-to-heart about boys. Aunt Betty was wearing a bright green strapless swimsuit and there were little bits of corn stuck in her teeth from the corn on the cob she was eating. Keep in mind, this was twenty-five years ago! But for The Talking Woman, it's as if it were yesterday.

All this from two pieces of shredded dental floss. Amazing, isn't it? And she's going to find her husband and tell this story, including every excruciating detail because that's what she does.

As she tells her husband this story about her dad and Aunt Betty, it's going to remind her of twenty other things. What will she do? The Talking Woman is going to have to talk about *those* things too, because she has no unexpressed thoughts.

The Talking Woman marries The Talking Man, doesn't she? No, she doesn't. She marries The Secret Agent Man. The Secret Agent Man never has anything to say. At least, not anything personal. He has thoughts and feelings, but no one knows what they are because . . . he's The Secret Agent Man. Every event of his day, no matter how big, means nothing, is forgotten, and is not shared with anyone. Everything personal that happens in his life is a secret.

This morning, in the motel in which he was staying, he was flossing his teeth, and the floss shredded. His left hand shot into the mirror, shattering the glass and cutting his hand badly. As he recoiled from the mirror impact, his right foot slipped into the toilet and got lodged in it and wouldn't come out.

Luckily, his cell phone was within reach, and he was able to call for help. The paramedics came and bandaged his hand. They also got his foot out of the toilet. It turned out that one of the paramedics was his best friend back in high school. Is he going to tell his wife what happened? Are you kidding? He's forgotten the whole incident by lunchtime.

His wife asks him that evening, "What happened to your hand?" He says, "Oh, nothing." Nothing? That's a lie! She presses him by saying, "Your hand is cut and you're limping." He replies, "It was just a little accident."

She thinks, "Well, duh! I know it was an accident." She says, "Go on." But, he won't go on. She shouldn't be surprised. He never goes on. He's not going to talk about it. No, of course he doesn't want to talk about it. It's a secret, and he's The Secret Agent Man. "I'm sorry, honey, but I'm Secret Agent 009. The information you're requesting is classified. It's a matter of National Security." Actually, it's *Personal* Security.

Who does he think his wife is? A spy? Now, if she is a spy, he'd better keep secrets. But if she's not, The Secret Agent Man needs to learn how to open up to her.

Not a Good Combination

As you can see, women and men are incredibly different from each other when it comes to communication. Most women are very comfortable with verbal intimacy and have a built-in craving for it. Most men are very uncomfortable with verbal intimacy and have a built-in drive to avoid it. Not a good combination for a relationship, is it?

When a woman sees a chance for intimacy in a conversation, she reacts as if someone has placed a wonderful gift basket in the room. It's a basket with an assortment of chocolates, bath oils and lotions, a gift certificate to her favorite store, and a coupon for a day spa. She throws herself at it. She can't wait to unpack all this terrific stuff!

When a man sees the possibility for intimacy in a conversation, he reacts as if someone has rolled a live grenade into the room. He leaps away from it in a desperate attempt to save himself!

The Secret Agent's Wall

Because of these differences, many married couples are not able to talk on anything but a superficial level. There is a huge, thick, seemingly impenetrable wall between the husband and the wife which prevents emotional connection.

This wall is erected and maintained by The Secret Agent Spouse. The Secret Agent Spouse could be the husband or the wife. The Talking Spouse knows how to express feelings and share on a deeper level. This spouse is ready, willing, and usually desperate to punch through the wall and experience emotional intimacy. The Secret Agent Spouse, however, stays behind the wall and simply refuses to allow any deeper level conversations to occur.

Did I Marry a Secret Agent Spouse?

I have developed a test that will confirm with one hundred-percent accuracy if you've married a Secret Agent. Although my test assumes that the husband is the Secret Agent, it could just as easily be the wife.

1. He is content with a very low level of intimacy
   in the marriage.   T F
2. He does not talk in a personal, heart-to-heart
   way with you.   T F

3. He holds his emotions and deep thoughts inside. T F
4. His idea of quality time is having you sit beside him while he watches television. T F
5. He seems to love his television, his computer, and his job more than he loves you. T F
6. He believes the only purpose of romance was to get you to marry him. T F
7. The only time he's passionate is when he wants—and during—sex. T F
8. He has the listening skills of a tree stump. T F
9. He's into conservation . . . conservation of words. He thinks there's no point in using twenty-five words when one or two will do. T F
10. You've come to realize that 99 percent of his entire conversational repertoire with you consists of these twenty statements/questions T F

"Fine."
"Okay."
"Pretty good."
"Sure."
"I don't know."
"Nothing's wrong."
"I don't want to talk about it."
"I said I was sorry."
"Get over it."
"You're overreacting."
"You shouldn't feel that way."
"I forgot."

"I never said that."

"It's that time of month, isn't it?"

"How about some sex, baby?"

"What's on television?"

"Do we have to visit your parents?"

"Where are my socks?"

"What's for dinner?"

"What did you say?"

11. He'd rather face a firing squad than talk through a conflict with you.   T   F
12. He does love you but cannot express love in ways that make you feel loved.   T   F
13. He's happy as long as you're giving him sex, food, clean clothes, and the remote control.   T   F
14. He thinks you have a great marriage.   T   F
15. He has no idea why you're upset and unhappy in the marriage.   T   F

If you answered True to at least ten of these, you're married to a Secret Agent.

Your Secret Agent Is Intimacy Challenged

Your Secret Agent isn't a bad guy. He's not evil or intentionally mean. He hasn't killed anyone. He doesn't run over squirrels for sport. He's a moral, decent, and upright person who works hard at his job. He's not having an affair. He's not an alcoholic or a drug user. He isn't addicted to anything. He does not verbally or physically abuse you. He's solid, stable, and responsible. He's a good guy! He even loves you. You know he loves you.

The one problem with him—and it is a big one—is that he doesn't show you love in the way you need to be shown love. He doesn't meet your deepest and most important need as a wife: to be emotionally connected to him. He doesn't open up and share himself with you. His feelings, his personal thoughts, his problems, his worries, his relationship with Jesus Christ, and his hopes and dreams all stay buried inside. He is intimacy challenged.

The one arena in which he seems to be able to give himself to you is sex. During foreplay and intercourse, he can be warm and sensitive and loving. But, frankly, that's not good enough. It's not good enough for you. You need him to give himself to you emotionally. Physical love without emotional connection is difficult—even painful—for you. And, it does not meet your greatest human relationship need.

You really and truly don't know your husband. And you desperately want—actually, need—to know him. That's why you got married—to be close to him! You need to know and experience who he really is inside. You need him to know and experience who you really are inside. But, that hasn't happened in your marriage, and it doesn't look as though it's ever going to happen.

The reason for this is that it takes two for true intimacy to happen. He must talk! He must put aside his logic and fears and self-protection and let his emotions come out. He will have to open up and share with you, regularly, his personal stuff. As a woman, you know this is true because you know how intimacy in a relationship works. But he doesn't get it. And he certainly isn't joining you in this intimacy process. You're still at Square One. Why? Because your Secret Agent won't talk on a personal level!

Your Secret Agent is emotionally stunted. He hides his true self behind his wall. He might be a pretty expressive guy with a great sense of humor. I've known Secret Agents who have no trouble talking. But they close down when it comes to any personal, below-the-surface conversation.

Oh, he'll talk to you. But only about things that are "safe" for him in his mind and are superficial: generalities about his day, facts and events, logical observations, financial matters, his job, his schedule, home maintenance, the kids, vacation plans. . . . These are the kinds of things he could share with anyone—a friend, his dad or mom or brother, the mail carrier. But, but . . . you're his *wife*! You need more than this!

The Secret to Dealing with a Secret Agent

Here's a dialogue that I've had in my therapy office with hundreds of spouses married to Secret Agents:

> Spouse: "Dr. Clarke, I've tried everything to get my spouse to open up and talk on a personal level—about himself, inside, his thoughts and feelings. Nothing has worked. It's going to take an act of God to change my spouse and get us emotionally connected."
>
> Dave Clarke: "You're right. You're more right than you know. Let me ask you some questions. First, what kind of spiritual bonding do you do as a couple?"
>
> Spouse: "Spiritual bonding? What do you mean?"
>
> Dave Clarke: "Do you have regular spiritual conversations in which each of you shares how you're doing in your relationship with God?"
>
> Spouse: "No. No, we don't."
>
> Dave Clarke: "Do you pray together regularly? And I don't mean at meal times. I mean praying together for five minutes at least three times a week."

Spouse: "No."

Dave Clarke: "Do you read the Bible together regularly and talk about how you're applying Scripture to your lives?"

Spouse: "No."

Dave Clarke: "Don't feel too bad. You and your spouse are in the majority. Very few married couples spiritually bond. This is for three main reasons. Your parents didn't model it for you. No one ever taught you how. Not many churches provide specific, how-to teaching about spiritually bonding as a couple. The secret to breaking through your Secret Agent's wall and becoming emotionally connected is the process of spiritual bonding. There are many avenues to intimacy, but the spiritual is the most important one. If you and your spouse will begin the process and move into spiritual bonding, you will receive two major benefits. One, by itself it will create the best and deepest passion possible between a husband and wife. Two, your spiritual bond will break through the wall and lead to emotional intimacy."

Spouse: "Spiritual intimacy is very private and personal. Do you think now is the right time for us to work on that? I mean, shouldn't we get emotional intimacy first, and then branch out to the spiritual?"

Dave Clarke: "Now—right now—is always the best time to include God in your lives and relationship. How have you done up to now, trying to emotionally bond first? We will work on some specific emotionally bonding behaviors, but the key is going to be your spiritual bonding. Real, deep emotional intimacy in a marriage never happens without God's presence and power. It does require faith to step forward and spiritually bond when you feel vulnerable, trust is low, and you don't feel ready to be that personal with your partner. And, it is unknown territory, and it will seem awkward and uncomfortable at first. If you step out and do it, God will reward you lavishly, and you will thank him forever."

Now, I'll teach you how to spiritually bond.

12

Put God Where He Belongs

Where is God in the Song of Solomon? Where is God in all this playfulness, flirtation, romance, and sexual pleasure? He's right in the middle of it. Literally.

Solomon (5:1a)
  "I have come into my garden, my sister, my bride;
  I have gathered my myrrh along with my balsam.
  I have eaten my honeycomb and my honey;
  I have drunk my wine and my milk."

The lovers have just completed a wonderful night of love-making. It is their wedding night, and they've enjoyed intercourse for the first time. Solomon, being the expressive guy he is, describes their intercourse with enthusiasm and wonder.

At this point, the exact center of the Song, someone speaks to both Solomon and Shulamith.

(5:1b)
"Eat, friends;
Drink and imbibe deeply, O lovers."

Who is this person? I believe it is God himself. Two experts on the Song, Dr. Craig Glickman, author of *Solomon's Song of Love* (New York: Howard Books, 2003), and Dr. Jack S. Deere in *The Bible Knowledge Commentary* (Colorado Springs: David C. Cook, 1989), also hold this view.

God does not step away when Solomon and Shulamith consummate their love. He is right there with them in the bedroom, happy for them and blessing their physical union and passion. It may seem incredible but God actually encourages them to experience as much passion and pleasure as they possibly can.

Since God is with the lovers during intercourse, he certainly wants to be with them at all times. He wants to join them everywhere they are together. He also blesses all aspects of their love. He approves all the actions Solomon and Shulamith take in the Song to create passion and intimacy.

Most of all, because it is recorded that God enters this love story right at the center of the book, he desires to be at the center of the marriage relationship. That is where he belongs. God is clearly at the center of Solomon and Shulamith's marriage. That's why they have such an amazingly passionate relationship.

Is he at the center of your marriage? Have you invited him not only into your hearts, but also into your marriage?

Who Is the Source of Passion in Marriage?

When God is at the center of a marriage, what happens? Here's what happens.

Shulamith (8:6a)
"Put me like a seal over your heart,
Like a seal on your arm.
For love is as strong as death,
Jealousy is as severe as Sheol . . ."

Passion happens! Shulamith tells Solomon she wants them to be inseparable and for their love to be strong and powerful. But she's not done yet.

Shulamith (8:7)
"Many waters cannot quench love,
Nor will rivers overflow it;
If a man were to give all the riches of his house for
love,
It would be utterly despised."

Wow! Shulamith describes their love as precious, priceless, and unable to be extinguished. Who wants a love like this? We all do!

The key to getting a love like this is found right at the center of Shulamith's wonderful expression of her feelings for Solomon.

Shulamith (8:6b)
"Its flashes are flashes of fire,
The very flame of the LORD."

Shulamith says the fire of the passionate love she and Solomon feel is the fire of *God*. God creates and continues to fuel their passion for each other.

We've all had human passion, haven't we? Because it's fueled by human strength, it's weak and never lasts. God is the source of true passion in marriage. It comes from him and only from him.

If we, as married couples, want a passion that is powerful and permanent, we have to do what Shulamith and Solomon do: put God at the center of the relationship, and keep him there.

To put God where he belongs in your marriage, you need to follow four passion principles.

Passion Principle #1: Come to Christ

As 1 Corinthians 15:3–4 makes clear, when you believe that Jesus Christ died on the cross for your sins and that Jesus literally rose from the dead, then you know God and you are a Christian. (If you want to know more about beginning a personal relationship with God through Jesus, please see appendix A in the back of this book.)

Once you both have a relationship with God, you can begin to share him as a *couple*. If your spouse is not a Christian yet, I still urge you to start a spiritual bonding process. Along the way, the non-Christian spouse may come to know God through Christ.

Passion Principle #2: Share Your Personal Spiritual Growth

Part of the spiritual bond Sandy and I have comes from our private, personal relationships with God. On our own, we each actively pursue a closer and richer walk with him. I have a daily quiet time in which I pray, read the Bible, meditate on what I read, and study a devotional. I talk to God throughout the day and serve him as he brings opportunity my way. Sandy works on her own spiritual life in many of these same ways.

We spiritually bond when we come *together* on a regular basis and share the personal growth we are experiencing. We do this during our couple talk times. I tell Sandy the insights I've gained from my Bible reading, how God is working in my life, and what I believe God wants me to learn in the next several months. Sandy then tells me what's going on in her spiritual life. This is deep, honest sharing, and it creates a powerful bond between us.

As I've grown spiritually, my marriage has blossomed. Seeking to be more like Christ has automatically made me a better husband. Rather than being threatened by Sandy's strong spiritual life, I'm now genuinely interested in what's happening between Jesus and her. And when I get a spiritual insight, or I see God moving in my life, Sandy is the first person I tell. We are sharing Christ these days, and he is blessing our marriage in too many ways to count.

If your marriage is like mine, you and your spouse will grow at different rates. That's okay. The important thing is that you're both growing. A big part of the spiritual bond I'm talking about is sharing the personal growth you each experience. Following the suggestions I have made for your own spiritual life will fill your reservoir of things to share with your spouse. You cannot share what you don't have.

Passion Principle #3: Pray Together

You can pray as a couple in many different, creative ways. The following practical guidelines can get you started.

Schedule three five-minute prayer times each week in your couple talk times. (I discussed the couple talk times in chapter four.) You can pray for the first five minutes of three of your scheduled 30-minute couple times. This not only makes fitting prayer into busy schedules more convenient, but it creates a deeper mood and warms you up for the conversation part of your couple time.

Choose one special place in your home to pray. Using the place where you have your couple times makes the most sense. After prayer, just stay where you are and move into conversation. This place must be private and quiet. Get the kids out of your hair. This is not family devotions; it's couple prayer time.

When you pray, hold hands. This connects you, and it is an outward expression of your one-flesh relationship.

Pray out loud. You're not spiritually bonding if you pray silently. Listening to your partner talk to God is an important part of sharing his or her bond with God. It is common for one spouse or sometimes both spouses to struggle with praying out loud. If you have not prayed out loud in another's presence, it will be a new and maybe uncomfortable experience at first. The spouse for whom the experience is the newest and perhaps is intimidating may pray silently for the first week or two. To indicate he or she is finished praying, the silent partner may just squeeze his or her partner's hand.

In the beginning, neither one of you will be praying on a deep, personal level. You may feel vulnerable and not completely at ease at first. You'll bring up topics that are important to you, but are not that deep and intimate. When you have prayed together for a while, you will gradually feel safe and increase your transparency in prayer. Make that a significant goal.

Husband, you may be too intimidated to pray in front of your wife. She talks better—and more—than you, and she probably will pray "better" than you will. She may be closer to God than you. The truth is, she won't ever criticize your prayers. After your first out-loud prayer with her, she will thank God for your words and for your courage. She will be happy and impressed beyond words that you are praying with her.

Make a list and take turns in prayer. Get a pad and jot down the requests you each want to bring before God. When you have a list, divide it up between you and pray one at a time. Here's a sample list one couple used during a prayer time:

> the church's missionary conference
> guidance for the pastors at church
> a friend's illness
> a possible promotion or increase in salary
> money to pay for college tuition
> the children:
>> Steve—his grade in science
>> Susan—wisdom and protection in her dating
>>> relationships
>> Carrie—more friends and a part-time job
> our marriage:
>> to spend more quality time together and for the
>>> Lord's leading in specific ways to do this
>> to keep praying three times a week
>> to have sex at least once a week

Your prayer list will also serve as a written record of God's faithfulness. As God answers your prayers, jot down the answers and the dates of the answers.

Spend a few minutes at each prayer session *praising God* for who he is and *always thank him* for what he has done and is doing for your family. God is worthy of praise and he loves to be worshiped in this way.

You'll find that you both will be more open and personal in what you say to God as you continue to pray together. You'll pray for your real concerns and the deep desires of your hearts. You'll share intimate things that you will never share with any other person.

Passion Principle #4: Read the Bible Together

The Bible is God's Word. That's right—God's actual Word! It is incredibly powerful. You can apply its power to your marriage by reading and studying and obeying it. Also, as a bonus, the Bible can cut through all the barriers between the two of you and bring you closer to each other than you have ever been.

> For the Word of God is living and active and sharper than any two-edged sword, and piercing as far as the division of soul and spirit, of both joints and marrow, and able to judge the thoughts and intentions of the heart.
>
> Hebrews 4:12

If this isn't a great description of intimacy, I don't know what is! If you read and study God's Word together, it will reveal who you really are. When two hearts are revealed, you have intimacy—an intimacy all the better and deeper because God gave it to you through his Word.

You can probably think of many helpful ways to read and study the Bible as a couple. I recommend you start by following this simple and effective plan: read on Monday, discuss on Friday.

Read on Monday

Sit down early in the week—we'll say Monday—and read out loud the passage of Scripture you have selected. Choose a brief passage—no more than three verses. Take a moment or two to silently meditate on the passage. Either out loud or silently ask God to speak to you through what you read from his Word.

Then take turns briefly discussing your response to the passage. What does it mean? What is God saying to you? What thoughts or emotions does the passage trigger in you? (This is not a process of learning deeper truths in the Bible or always getting answers to hard questions. That comes through study of the Bible, through weekly classes and group studies and sermons.)

At the end of this meeting, do three things:

Schedule a time to discuss the passage on Friday.

Pray together, out loud, that God will speak to you both over the next four or five days through the passage you read.

Each of you write the passage on a three-by-five card. Over the next few days, agree to read the passage at least once a day and meditate on it. You could make this brief meditation part of your personal, daily quiet time with the Lord. You are preparing for Friday!

As you meditate and pray for insight from God, jot down on the back of your card what you think God is impressing on your mind and heart about the verse. By Friday, you'll each have a few notes written down.

Discuss on Friday

On Friday, meet again to share the results of the meditation and reflection. At this second meeting, you'll both have more to say.

Read what you've written on the back of your three-by-five cards. You may share what the passage means for your individual life, marriage, family, career, or your service in your local church. Maybe God is confronting you through the passage. Maybe God wants you to apply the passage in a certain way in the following week.

Can you see how this plan has the power to create some stimulating spiritual conversations? God will speak to you through the passages you select, and by sharing this intimate spiritual information with your spouse, you will be drawn closer together.

You don't have to do this every week. No couple is that spiritually minded. Besides, who has the time for that? I recommend this Monday–Friday plan once every two months. Go ahead, try this "read on Monday, discuss on Friday" plan. You'll like it. I know God will like it, and he'll bless you for your reading and discussing and obeying his precious Word. If you want to get a complete picture of spiritual intimacy in marriage, read my book, *A Marriage After God's Own Heart*.

When you bond spiritually as a couple, two wonderful things happen. One, you get the best and the deepest passion possible between a husband and a wife. Strictly by itself, coming together as a couple spiritually produces a passion and an energy unmatched in any other area of heterosexual intimacy.

Two, your growing spiritual intimacy energizes your emotional and physical passion. As you connect to God as a couple, he gives you a healthy, vibrant passion in all three areas of intimacy: spiritual, emotional, and physical. With God as its source, your passion for each other will never be exhausted. Never.

13

Unforgiven

Conflict is an inevitable part of every marriage. I mean, what do you expect when you put a man and a woman together in the same living space? Constant harmony and peace? I don't think so. Couples who learn how to handle conflict successfully give themselves a wonderful opportunity to enjoy passionate, intimate marriages. Couples who do not learn how to handle conflict successfully give themselves a wonderful opportunity—in fact, a guaranteed opportunity—to never enjoy passion and intimacy in their marriages.

Because conflict is such an important area, I'm devoting three chapters to it. In this chapter, I give you an unpleasant glimpse at the damage unresolved conflict—and the resentments it causes—can wreak on a marriage. In the following chapter, I illustrate the classic mistakes most couples make when facing conflict. Finally, using principles from the Song, I teach you how to resolve in a healthy way the conflicts that inevitably arise in marriages.

If Resentment Stays, Love Goes

The wife and her husband settled in on my couch. It was my first therapy session with them. They were in their mid- to late-thirties, had been married almost fifteen years, and had two children. Both said they knew Jesus Christ personally and were actively involved in a local church. When I asked them why they'd come to see me, it became clear very quickly that they had no idea how to effectively handle conflict. And because of that, there were many resentments simmering just beneath the surface of their marriage.

The husband told me I'd have to find out from his wife why they were there, because he didn't have a clue. I thought to myself, "You're right, buddy. You don't have a clue." I knew exactly what he was going to say next. I could have mouthed the words right along with him. He gave me the same little speech that hundreds of clueless husbands have delivered in my office. Here it is, with the addition of my editorial comments—things I thought but did not say.

He Just Doesn't Get It

Husband: "I'm happy in our marriage."

Me: ("Well, that's great for you. Isn't there someone else in this marriage?")

Husband: "We're doing fine."

Me: ("If you say so, it must be true.")

Husband: "We have a good life. We make a good income, we have a nice home, good investments, two vacations a year, great friends, two super kids, a terrific church, and our health."

Me: ("Ah, the American Dream! Guess what? A good life doesn't equal a good marriage. Funny thing—you didn't mention mutual respect or love or passion or intimacy.")

Husband: "I'm a good husband. I don't drink, go to bars, do drugs, beat her, or have affairs. I work hard, provide for my family, attend church, and take care of the yard and the cars."

Me: ("No one is questioning your character. You're a good guy, not a monster. I'll grant you that. But being a good husband requires communication skills, romance, and spiritual attentiveness. God doesn't say, 'Don't be a monster.' God says, 'Husbands, love your wives as Christ loved the church' [Eph. 5:25].")

Husband: "I'm not the most romantic guy in the world."

Me: ("Translation: 'I'm just about the least romantic guy in the world.'")

Husband: "We have a good sex life."

Me: ("Translation: 'I get sex whenever I want it.' Sex might be good for you, but I doubt if it is good for your wife.")

Husband: "My wife is a good woman. She takes care of all my needs. She cleans the house, does the laundry, cooks the meals, and takes care of the kids."

Me: ("It sounds as though you're describing Betty Crocker or Martha Stewart. Or your *mother*. And, it's still about *you*. How about your wife and her needs? What do you do for her?")

Husband: "We're older now, and so our love isn't the passionate, intense kind we had back when we first got together. It's a solid, committed, and comfortable love."

Me: ("What are you, ninety years old? It sounds as though you're talking about an old shoe. Committed is good, but committed plus romance and excitement and emotional closeness is much better. That's what God desires for you.")

Husband: "I love my wife."

Me: ("No, you don't love her. Not by God's definition. And not by her definition. Love is something you *do*.")

Husband: "We don't have any marriage problems. We don't need a psychologist."

I did speak after this last comment. I almost said, "Sir, if you have no marriage problems, why are you in my office?" Fortunately, with great effort, I bit my tongue. What I did say was, "Thanks for sharing. That's *your* view, and I understand how you see things. Now, let's hear from your wife, the other, and equal part of your marriage."

She Didn't Help Him to Get It

The wife looked uncomfortable as she prepared to talk about her marriage. She fidgeted, smoothed out her dress a few times, and shot nervous glances at her husband and me. I knew—I just knew—she was going to deliver the standard, "I'll nibble around the edges of my unhappiness and ask for changes without making him angry or hurt, 'sweet little wife,' state of the marriage" address. And, that's exactly what she did. Below are her words, with my unspoken thoughts:

Wife: "Honey, first of all, I want you to know you are a really good husband."

Me: ("No, he's not! The man's not meeting your very deep, God-ordained needs. Please. I'm begging you. Don't list all his good points as a husband—not now.")

Wife: "It would be hard to list all your good points as a husband, but let me try. You work hard, you provide the money we need to live, you're a great dad, you help around the house, you don't drink or engage in other behavior that would harm the kids and me, you take care of the cars, you keep the yard looking beautiful . . ."

Me: ("I think I'm going to throw up. You're dying inside because you have no emotional connection to this man you really love. Yet, you are telling him—and me—that at least when you look out the window, the yard is gorgeous! I bet you wouldn't mind having the most scraggly, weed-infested yard in the neighborhood if you could have just two or three deep, personal conversations a week with your husband. Please. Tell him that!")

Wife: "I love you, honey. And I know you love me. We have a good life together."

Me: ("Stop calling him honey! Call him by his name! Don't say you love him and that he loves you. That's not what he needs to hear. You're being too nice! You're ignoring your pain and acting as though it does not exist.")

Wife: "But, there are a few things in our marriage I want to see improve. Over the past few years especially, I just haven't felt like we . . ."

Me: ("Too late. Don't bother. You took too long getting to the 'but' part. Your husband's not going to listen to your real concerns and pain. Why should he? You just spent five minutes complimenting him and confirming what he already believes: he's a good husband, you have a good life together, and what in the world are we doing in this shrink's office? If you were a boss and you were telling an employee how he should improve his job performance, maybe you would begin by telling him about his good points. But this is a very different situation. Your very happiness and fulfillment in this marriage and the marriage itself are at stake.")

Just as she tentatively tiptoed into telling her husband about the weak areas of their marriage, he glanced at me with a little smirk on his face. His look said it all: "See Doc, what did I tell you? You heard her. We're okay. She may have a few minor beefs, but our marriage is strong. It's fine. I'm a good husband in the most important areas." With her husband only half-listening, she shared what she thought was wrong with their marriage.

"Our main problem is communication. We talk not about important areas but only unimportant things—superficial, mundane, mechanical things: home improvements, our jobs, the kids' activities and schedules, and what our parents are doing. We don't sit down together, look at each other, and really talk. He doesn't open up and share on a personal level with me. I want to know who he is and what he's thinking and feeling. I want to share his inner life, his heart, not just the outside him. I love him. I'm glad I married him. He's good to me. But I don't know him. I want intimate, deep conversations that will lead to real closeness. We get along, but I want more than that. I don't know . . . maybe I'm asking for too much. None of my girlfriends have this kind of emotional connection with their husbands, either. I'd also like us to learn how to work through conflicts. Honey, please don't clam up and walk away when we have something difficult or painful to discuss. When you do that, it leaves me hanging. I want to talk out my feelings with you and reach some kind of a resolution that will help our love keep growing. When you refuse to face the conflict, all my emotions stay bottled up inside, and it hurts me. Plus, that way we can't work out any solution or compromise. Life just goes on. I think you forget about the issue. But I don't."

At this point in the session, I sensed that this lady had a big pool of smoldering resentments. I could feel the anger percolating in her. I tried to tap it by asking, "It makes you really angry when he won't deal with a conflict, doesn't it?" She responded, a little too quickly, "Oh, no. Not angry. Just hurt and a little disappointed."

I thought to myself again, "Baloney. You're angry, all right. It's buried deep, but it's there." I tried again, this time out loud: "I think all the missed opportunities for conversation, the lack of emotional intimacy, and his refusal to allow you to express yourself in conflicts have created resentments inside you. I don't think you want these resentments, but I think you have them."

She looked shocked and stammered back, "No! No, no, no. I don't resent my husband. I do get hurt and frustrated and feel he is abandoning me when we don't talk personally or deal with a conflict. But these feelings go away. I think you're misunderstanding me. Our marriage is good. I just want it to be better."

I could have said, "Stop saying your marriage is good. Every time you say that, you reinforce your husband's belief that you don't need therapy, that you are happy with him, and that your marriage doesn't require any changes, or any changes of any real significance, anyway. The case you just gave for improving your marriage is weak and didn't even get close to getting your husband's attention.

"Your comments were way too general and way too nice and sweet. There was no punch. No urgency. No emotion. I got the impression you were talking about someone else's marriage that could stand a little improvement. This is *your* marriage, and you're not paying me all this money an hour to tell me you're doing well and just want a few changes. You're smiling on the outside and dying on the inside.

"When your husband won't meet your important, God-given needs, it hurts and angers you. *Every single time* he fails to meet your needs. And when you aren't even allowed to vent those feelings, they turn into resentment, even depression. You're still able to stuff these resentments down deep. You're not even aware you have them, but often you have an empty feeling, a feeling of missed joy. But these feelings are there, and if I can't get you to tap into them and express them directly to your husband, they will eventually destroy your respect and love for him. It's already happening, and you don't even realize it."

I could have said these things, but I didn't. At least, not right then. The therapy hour was up, and it wouldn't have done any good, anyway. This wife was not ready to admit that her marriage was lousy and that she was hanging on to some heavy-duty resentments against her husband and deep feelings of loss in the marriage. I went to Plan B and scheduled individual therapy sessions for the next week. Sometimes, I can get through to a spouse when I see him or her alone.

"She'll Get Over It, Doc"

I had forty-five minutes to convince this husband that his marriage was in serious trouble and changes were necessary. As he sat down, I said, "I want you to listen to me for the next fifteen minutes. Listen closely. You have a serious problem on your hands. I'm taking off the kid gloves, and I'm going to give it to you straight." Here's a brief summary of the points I hammered home:

"This is your second session at a Christian psychologist's office. Your wife asked you to come to therapy. There's no way she'd do that unless she was really hurting and because of this, very concerned about your marriage.

"You're an emotional stick. Like a lot of husbands, you keep all your deep feelings and thoughts locked away inside. You don't talk on a personal, self-disclosing level with your wife. You don't talk to her about what's really going on in your life, your career, your spiritual walk with God, your relationship with her, and your hopes and dreams and fears and vulnerabilities.

"From the history I took of your childhood in our first session, I know why you're a stick. Your dad's a stick. He taught you to clam up and stuff everything personal way down deep. Your mom put up with it, so you expect your wife to put up with it.

"You're not obeying God's instructions to husbands. You're not loving her the Ephesians 5:25 way, which is loving her in the same way Christ loved the church. You're not loving her in the 1 Peter 3:7 way, which is treating her gently, and tenderly meeting her needs. You're not loving her the Song of Solomon way, which is loving her with great passion and romance. You're not loving her the Ephesians 5:23–24 and John 13:3–5 ways, which is by serving her. You're loving her *your* way, not God's way.

"I know from our first session that your sex life as a couple isn't full of passion and excitement and intimacy. In fact, from your wife's perspective, it's boring and routine. I'm telling you here and now, that's *your* fault. Your wife cannot respond sexually unless she is emotionally connected to you. Your sex life is pretty poor, isn't it? How would it be for you if there were no sex at all? That's in your future if you don't change and become a better husband.

"Your wife's *number one need* in your marriage is to feel close to you. She wants and needs to experience life *together*, not as two separate persons. To have the Genesis 2:24 'one flesh' relationship God desires for every married couple, you must learn to open up and share personally with her on a regular basis. As long as you are a stick, you won't meet this critical need in her life.

"Over the years, you've hurt your wife again and again by being a stick. I know you haven't meant to, but you have. Every time you clammed up and chose not to share personally, you hurt her. Every time you avoided talking through a conflict, you hurt her. Every time you failed to romance her, you hurt her. And all those hurts are still there, inside of her. They've turned into resentments and are eating away at her love for you. If she doesn't express them soon, she'll hit the wall and have no feelings for you at all."

After firing all these verbal bullets, I sat back and waited for his angry, defensive, and rationalization-filled response. I wasn't disappointed. He said that the terrible picture I painted of his marriage wasn't even close to the truth.

He said, "Look, things aren't that serious. I know I can be a better husband, but I'm doing a good job. Nobody's perfect. She's a little upset now, but it'll pass. I know my woman. She'll get over it, Doc. She always does."

And then he added the real kicker, the statement that revealed why he thought his marriage was fine: "Doc, you're saying we're in serious trouble, but *she's* not saying that. You heard her in that first session. She's not angry. She's not letting me have it. She may want some improvements, but she's not telling me she resents me."

I replied, "I know she's not letting you have it. But, believe me, she has big time resentments against you. She's stuffing them and faking it with you. Like most wives, she finds it very difficult to express anger, deep hurt, and resentments with you. One day, she'll be through with faking, and she'll turn completely away from you. Her resentments will drive her to give up on you and move on rather than just live within the cold, emotionless, romanceless cell you put her in. You have a small window of opportunity to act and stop her from writing you off. So, you'd better get to work."

I urged him to quickly do three things: One, call his mother and have a heart to heart talk about what it was really like living with his dad, the original stick. Two, work to change as a husband, and love his wife the way *she* needs to be loved. Three, encourage—push, if necessary—his wife to express directly to him all her resentments.

He refused all three action steps. He just couldn't see what all the fuss was about. He told me, "I know you mean well, Doc, but all this psychobabble isn't for us. When you see her in her session tomorrow, I'm sure you'll realize that she's not all that upset."

Good Wives Don't Get Angry, Do They?

Well, so far I was zero for one. Now I had forty-five minutes to convince this wife that it was essential that she get in touch with her resentments and express them directly to her husband. I knew something she didn't know: her marriage was at stake. I went after her with these arguments:

"You are filled with anger and hurt at your husband. All of his insensitive behaviors have led to a big pool of resentments inside. Don't tell me he's a good husband. He's a lousy husband! Don't tell me you've forgiven him for not meeting your most important needs. You haven't! To forgive, you must first express the pain directly to the one who caused it.

"If you don't get your resentments out, even if he genuinely changed as a husband, it wouldn't make any difference to you. It wouldn't be enough because the resentments would outweigh his improvements. Every mistake he made would energize the resentment pool.

"But I wouldn't worry about him changing. If you won't be honest and tell him your resentments, he won't realize how serious things are, how bad you really feel. He'll keep thinking what he's thinking now—that your marriage is fine and dandy. So, he won't change. He has no reason to do anything differently! And, that's your fault.

"Your unexpressed resentments will limit your ability to be a good wife. You'll be irritable and impatient with him; you won't be supportive and encouraging; you won't be a responsive sex partner; you'll overreact and be nastier in conflicts; and you won't meet his needs.

"Worst of all, it's very likely your resentments will kill your feelings of respect and love for him. The day will come when you are completely numb toward him. You won't care about him, and you'll want out of the marriage. Don't look so shocked. It's already happening to you. You haven't hit the wall yet, but you're awfully close. You're playing the part of a good, Christian woman. But it's a façade! You're hiding your feelings and not stating them."

She admitted that she did have "some anger, hurt, and resentment" because of her needs not being met by her husband. "But," she said, "it isn't that much and I don't want to express these feelings to him." Here are her four reasons for this and my responses:

Wife: "Expressing anger and resentments just isn't Christian."

Me: "No, it *is* Christian. The Bible teaches us to 'speak the truth in love' (Eph. 4:15), to 'be angry, and yet do not sin' (Eph. 4:26), not to lie (Eph. 4:25), and to deal directly with anyone with whom we have an unresolved issue (Matt. 5:23–24)."

Wife: "But telling him how I really feel wouldn't be acting in a respectful way."

Me: "Quite the opposite. A big part of being respectful is being honest with your husband. Your job is to be honest with him. How can he be a good husband if he doesn't know what you need? Plus, your buried resentments will build up over time."

Wife: "I'm scared of my anger. If you're right, and my anger is pretty intense, I don't know if I can handle expressing it. I don't like being angry or showing anger. I was raised not to be angry, because it leads to damaged relationships."

Me: "Okay, now we're getting to the real reasons. It will be difficult and scary to express your internalized anger. But you can do it, and you will not drop dead or turn into a crazy woman. You'll clean out the anger inside, and you will feel much better. You need to be much *more* scared of the anger you *don't* express. It will do tremendous damage to you, your husband, and your marriage."

Wife: "If I dump on my husband all this anger and resentment you say I have, he'll be hurt. He'll probably get angry back at me. He'll be offended and pull further away from me."

Me: "He will be hurt, angry, and offended. I sure hope he is. Husbands only change when you scare them, rattle their cages, rock their worlds, and get their attention. He's like all the sticks I've seen. He wants your marriage to stay the way it is now and will change only if he has to. When he feels your genuine hurt and anger and knows you will not continue to accept the way things are, then he'll change. He doesn't see any need to change. Because you have not been honest with him, he does not know you are suffering. If you vent your resentments and longings, he'll see how serious things are and be motivated to make changes. He'll finally get it."

I urged her to write a letter to her husband. A letter with all her resentments and unfulfilled dreams in living color. No holding back. *The truth. In love.* I asked her to write as much as she needed. If she wrote forty pages, so be it. I told her I'd ask her to read it at our next marital session.

I could tell by the look on her face that she wasn't going to do it. She said her pastor and a well-known Christian author she was reading had recommended a different approach: to forget the past, pray, and quickly forgive her husband. Then, she was advised to focus on loving her husband unconditionally. She was told that eventually he'd come around and be the husband she'd always dreamed he'd be. She thanked me for my time and said she wouldn't need any more of my services.

I felt like saying, "This approach you're going to try is the same approach you've been trying for years. How is it going?" But I wished her well and said to call me if she changed her mind.

I Hate It When I'm Right

Ten months later, this same couple was sitting in front of me. But, oh, what a difference! The husband had called to make the appointment. He was sitting on the edge of my couch, nervous and sweating. The wife looked like a totally different woman. She was as cold as an Arctic blast. Her face was expressionless. She showed no emotion except for irritation that she was in my office. I thought to myself, "She's hit the wall."

She opened her mouth and said exactly what I thought she'd say. She wanted out of the marriage. She had finally gotten sick and tired of living with this man. She had no feelings for him at all. She just didn't care about him, period. She'd only come today to try and get it through his thick skull that it was over between them. She had gotten an apartment. She had gotten her own checking account. She had gotten an attorney. He'd be getting the divorce papers shortly. All she wanted from him was a friendly divorce.

Her husband was devastated, a shell of his former, confident self. He finally "got it," but it was too late. He told me through his tears, "Doc, you were right. I wish I had listened." I saw him in about ten individual sessions, and he did a lot of good work. He changed, as a man and as a husband.

But she could have cared less. Her resentments were still all inside, and they drove her away from him. She never came back to therapy after that session. She never wavered. She divorced him.

14 ·

The Little Dog, Conflict, and Me

Some time ago, I decided I needed a new exercise program. I had been using an exercise bicycle for years, and frankly, it was boring me silly. Pedaling and staring at the wall had gotten very old.

When I crabbed to Sandy, she said, "Why don't you walk in the neighborhood? All the experts say walking is the best exercise." I knew immediately that her idea was a winner. I took her in my arms, gave her several lingering kisses, and said, "Brilliant, Sweetie Carkst! I married a genius!"

Walking turned out to be an ideal aerobic activity for me. Ah, the great outdoors! The fresh, cool air. The quiet. The dew on the grass. The sun coming up on a brand new day. The chance to think and pray as I strolled briskly around my peaceful neighborhood.

Monday through Friday, I left my house at sunrise and walked for thirty minutes. Other than a few other early morning walkers, I was alone. It was the perfect way to start the day.

For two solid months, everything was perfect. I fantasized about pushing my exercise bicycle over a cliff, watching it shatter on the rocks below. I was never going to ride that torture machine again! I wasn't even going to donate it. Why inflict that kind of suffering on someone else?

But, then one day, it all changed. My beautiful, idyllic walking program was ruined by . . . *the little dog*. On that fateful morning, I was halfway through my walk. I was just passing a small, well-kept green and white house. Suddenly, a little dog burst from around the side of the house, running at me full speed and barking its head off.

I was shocked. Stunned. And—I'm not ashamed to confess—scared. Okay, I am ashamed to confess it. Instinctively, I sprinted down the street. I was sure the little dog was going to bite me. It didn't seem to be frothing at the mouth, but it may have had rabies.

After breaking the world record for one hundred meters, I looked back. The little dog had stopped in the middle of the street about fifty feet from its house. It was still barking and holding its head up in an arrogant pose. I could have sworn it had an evil little smile on its face. With one final bark, it trotted triumphantly back to its hiding place.

As I continued my walk, I experienced a series of intense emotions. First, relief. I was safe. Second, embarrassment. A tiny, scrawny, no-bigger-than-a-shoe-box dog had chased me—a grown man—down the street. If it had been a Doberman pinscher or a pit bull, my manhood wouldn't have taken such a blow. But this was a froufrou dog! You know, the kind of little dog that rich women carry around. The kind that wears ribbons and little plaid sweaters!

Third, anger. More like red-hot rage. How dare this little yipper dog destroy my wonderful walking routine and humiliate me in my own neighborhood! The nerve! The gall! I was furious at the little dog. I was also furious at myself for running away like a girl.

I considered my options. I could call Animal Control and have them waiting as I walked by the beast's house. There is a leash law in this county, after all. The Animal Control officers would scoop up the little dog and put him in the back of their truck. I'd look through the bars and say, "Well, I win, and you lose. Have a nice stay in the Big House. I hope you get along with some of the big dogs there. Did you actually think you could beat me?"

I could change my walking route. If I didn't pass its house, it couldn't chase me. There were no other dogs running around loose. Yes, I'd just choose a different route, and no one would ever know.

After some thought, I rejected these possibilities as being too cowardly. No, I'd have to think of something else. I couldn't allow a little dog to defeat me. After all, I was a human with a bigger brain!

My initial solution to this "conflict" was good old denial. I figured this unfortunate incident was just a crazy, unexplainable, onetime event. I chose to believe there wasn't a problem. I acted as though nothing had happened. I continued to walk my regular route.

This seemed to work. One more week went by, and the little dog was nowhere in sight. My confidence grew each time I passed its house. Maybe the miserable nuisance died of meanness. I looked for a simple, wooden cross but didn't spot it. But, suddenly, on the eighth day, the dog came tearing around the corner and chased me down the street again! This little dog was diabolically clever. It let me walk unmolested for a week so I would think the threat was over.

My next step was avoidance. I decided not to deal with the situation. I steered clear of the dog by not walking at all. I actually went back to the dreaded exercise bicycle.

After a week, I got my nerve up and went back to my walking route. "This is my neighborhood," I fumed, "and no four-legged canine is going to run me out of it." The very first day back on my route, the little dog rushed me. And I ran again.

That was the turning point in this man versus dog battle. I'd finally had enough. I'd stuffed my anger long enough, and the resentment against the little dog was boiling over. This neighborhood wasn't big enough for both of us.

I set out the next morning with a grim smile on my face. This was the day I would reclaim my lost manhood. It was mano-a-doggie time, and I intended to come out on top. I walked assertively right by the little dog's driveway. In fact, I actually stepped on the driveway, daring the menace to do something about it.

It waited until I was barely past the property line before making its mad, barking dash at me. I coolly turned and sprinted directly at the little dog, waving my hands and yelling at the top of my voice. The little dog was gutsy, I'll give it that. It kept coming at me until I was about ten feet away. Then, it realized I wasn't stopping. It lurched to a halt, yelped pitifully, and scurried back behind its house. I laughed out loud and long, as my nemesis ran with its tail between its little, spindly legs. Victory was sweet! I was on top of the world! The little dog has never again showed its face on my walks.

I've told this story for three reasons. One, I like telling it. Two, to prove that no little froufrou dog can get the best of me. Three, to serve as an illustration of many of the classic mistakes spouses make when faced with conflict.

Classic Mistakes in a Conflict

Marital conflict isn't pretty. The main reason it's not pretty is that each spouse has an incorrect, dysfunctional way of dealing with conflict. No one has a naturally healthy, effective way of dealing with conflict. In my little dog story, I covered a number of these dysfunctional styles of conflict resolution. See if you recognize yours.

The Great Denier

This is the spouse (usually the husband) who, after a fight, acts as though nothing has happened. You sleep like a baby and carry on the next morning as if no conflict had ever taken place. "Fight? What fight?" It's a masterful acting job. You have a roomful of Academy Awards for your performances. But you have no awards for your ability to work through conflicts.

The Master of Avoidance

In this style, you simply choose not to talk about the conflict. You don't pretend it didn't happen; you just refuse to dialogue about it. The beauty of this strategy is that your spouse cannot make you talk. You control with your silence.

The Winner

When a conflict erupts, you immediately see it as a competition to be won. And you intend to be the winner. The man thinks he's right because of his *logic*. He has reasoned it out and can prove his case with cold, hard facts. The woman thinks she's right because of her emotion. She *feels* very strongly about her position, so she must be right.

I say: "Baloney to both of you!" In the vast majority of marital conflicts, there are *two* opinions. Two ways of looking at the situation. Two truths. It's not a matter of who's right and who's wrong. You both are right! It's a matter of understanding each other's point of view.

The Escape Artist

You can't stand conflict. You loathe it. You're scared of it. You'll do anything to get away from it. So, you run at the first sign of conflict with your spouse. You have a sudden urge to go to the bathroom, and you leave the room. You leave the house. You jump into your car and drive away. You hang up the phone. The problem with this is, when you return, your spouse and the conflict are still there.

The Screaming Meemie

Just like the little dog in my story, you are way too aggressive in a conflict. You raise your voice. You get too angry. You talk over your partner. You say mean, hurtful things. You're not aware of how intense you become in a conflict. You make it impossible for your spouse to engage you in a reasonable, respectful dialogue about the issue.

The Stuffer

You are very uncomfortable with your anger, so you stuff it down when a conflict occurs. Even though you have anger and other real feelings, time after time you stuff them deep inside. You usually let your spouse get his or her way. You say, "Oh, no, I'm not angry." "I don't mind if you do it that way." "I don't have an opinion one way or the other."

If you're a Stuffer, all the percolating resentments inside you will come out in one of three ways. One, you'll become depressed. Two, you'll lose your love for your spouse. Three, you'll periodically explode in anger at your spouse. This can happen when there seems no reason for it, which confuses your spouse, because you did not show this anger when it was appropriate. You've got to find a way to release your anger in a healthy way.

—⁂—

My little dog story does not contain an exhaustive list of ineffective conflict resolution styles. I don't want to leave anyone out, so here are some more to choose from.

The Pushy Spouse

You want to talk the conflict out and resolve it as soon as humanly possible. The conflict must be resolved, and it must be resolved *now*. Once a conflict occurs, you will talk about nothing else until it's resolved to your satisfaction. You will follow your spouse around the house and continue to talk about the conflict. You don't care whether your spouse wants to talk about the issue or not. You are a royal pain! You are a nag! Without realizing it, you are the one who prolongs the conflict.

The Talking Spouse

I don't know how to say this politely, so I'll just say it. You talk too much in a conflict. You bury your spouse in an avalanche of words. You use too much detail. You overanalyze the situation. You don't give your spouse an opportunity to process what you've said and to respond. It's okay to be an expressive person, but you must learn to condense your material.

The Defensive Spouse

You are very sensitive and touchy in a conflict. When your spouse speaks about something you've said or done, you instantly feel defensive and fire back a verbal missile. "That's not true!" "I never meant to make you feel that way!" "I'm the one who should be angry here!" "Oh, yeah? Well how about the time you _____?"

The Martyr Spouse

When your spouse brings up a conflict issue, you immediately—and usually sarcastically—take the blame. "I just can't do anything right, can I?" "I can't please you." "You're right again, and I'm wrong." This is a strategy to distract your spouse from the real issue and to avoid taking any responsibility for what happened.

The Sorry Spouse

You think the words "I'm sorry" will magically make the conflict disappear. You don't want to go through the painful process of talking through the conflict. So you offer a quick "I'm sorry" and hope it will all go away. When that doesn't work, you whine, "But I said I was sorry! What more do you want?" What your spouse wants—and needs—is to actually talk about the conflict and reach understanding and closure.

The Moving-on Spouse

You don't like to face conflict, so you use the excuse that "it's all in the past." You say to your spouse, "Honey, why are you bringing up the past? That's ancient history. It happened, and there's nothing we can do about it now. We just have to move on. Stop living in the past." The truth is, it's not in the past until you talk it out together. Saying "It's in the past" will not remove the feelings and hurts that are connected to the conflict.

The Power of Unresolved Conflicts

All these dysfunctional styles of dealing with conflict prevent you from resolving conflict in a healthy way. All—and I do mean all—your conflicts remain and fester inside each of you. These pools of resentment push you apart and energize all your ongoing conflicts.

When you have a conflict today, it is not just about that conflict. It's about all your unresolved conflicts from the past too. Your unresolved conflicts transfer or carry over to every new conflict. The feelings aroused in a conflict are compounded by those of past conflicts that were never really resolved. This makes it very difficult, if not impossible, to work through any conflict.

Your unresolved conflicts do great damage to your marriage. They prevent you from continuing to engage in positive behavior. They lead to largely separate lives. They kill your love for each other.

All right, enough bad news. The good news is, the two of you can learn how to successfully resolve your conflicts. You can resolve your current, ongoing conflicts and clean out your pools of past, unresolved conflicts.

Let's consult our Marriage Enrichment experts, Solomon and Shulamith. They knew how to deal effectively with conflict, and they can show you how.

15

Face Conflict, Deal with It, and Make Up after It

Solomon and Shulamith have a wonderful relationship. It's spontaneous. Playful. Intimate. Passionate. But, it's not a perfect relationship. In Song of Solomon 5:2–7:13, we read the story of a conflict between these two lovers. It's not a minor disagreement, either. It's a doozy of a conflict!

I find this lengthy passage very refreshing. When I read these verses for the first time, I said out loud, "Yes! They're fighting! It's about time!" Solomon and Shulamith's nasty, petty fight helps me relate to them. They're real people in a real marriage. The conflict they have is just like the kind of fights Sandy and I have. It's just like the kind of fights you and your spouse have.

In addition to being a refreshing burst of realism, Solomon and Shulamith's conflict is instructive. They know how to effectively resolve conflict and get their love relationship back on track. Most of us as couples don't know how to do this. No one ever taught us how. God wants us to learn how from the example of Solomon and Shulamith.

Trouble in Paradise

Their conflict comes out of nowhere. It is shocking. Totally unexpected. It is their wedding night, and Solomon and Shulamith have just had intercourse for the first time (5:1). Talk about an incredible high! What could go wrong? Actually, anything and everything could go wrong. They're married now, remember?

In 5:2–3, Solomon wants to make love to Shulamith, but she rejects him. The poor guy knocks on the bedroom door, and she ignores him. She's comfortable in bed and doesn't want to be bothered. Don't you just love this? It's a classic scenario as old as marriage. The husband asks for sex, and the wife says no.

In 5:4–6a, Solomon leaves. Even though he must be bummed out and deflated, he maintains his composure and doesn't make a scene. I wish I had that kind of self-control.

Shulamith, in 5:6b, realizes her mistake and goes after Solomon immediately. She has no good reason for rejecting his sexual advances and feels tremendous guilt. She searches for him, calls his name, but he's nowhere to be found.

Shulamith continues to pursue Solomon despite being physically assaulted by the night watchmen (5:7). The trauma of being beaten up does not stop her from trying to find Solomon. She's going to track him down and fix their conflict no matter what. She has hurt him and will do whatever it takes to win back his trust.

Right in the middle of the conflict, Shulamith verbalizes a long list of Solomon's positive qualities (5:10–16). You've got to be kidding me! Not to be left out, Solomon comes right back with a long list of Shulamith's positive qualities (6:4–9). Shouldn't they be listing only each other's negative qualities? That's what we do, isn't it?

When you and your spouse are right in the middle of a conflict, do you force yourselves to think about and verbalize the positives about each other? Of course not. Solomon and Shulamith know they can't resolve conflict by focusing only on the problem. They know they have to deal with the conflict, but they also know they can soften their anger and rekindle their feelings of love by remembering the wonderful things about each other. Thinking about each other's positive qualities actually helps prepare them to work through the conflict.

Finally, in 7:1–13, their conflict ends the way all marital conflicts ought to end: with makeup sex! They have worked through the issue and want to seal their reconciliation with intercourse, a supreme way of showing and feeling love. They have come together emotionally and now want to come together physically.

The Seven Steps of Conflict Resolution

What can we learn about conflict from the experience of Solomon and Shulamith? To teach you to effectively resolve conflict, I'm going to cover seven steps. Some of these steps are in the Song and some are not. The steps that are not specifically taught in the Song are God's truths also, I believe, and will help you achieve the Song's goal for marital conflict: face it, deal with it, and make up after it.

Step one: Schedule a discussion

When a conflict erupts, you are not ready to talk about it. Anger and hurt are intense, and you will say and do things you'll regret. Certainly, as the Song teaches, you are to pursue your spouse immediately in an attempt to begin the process of working through the problem. However, that doesn't mean you launch right into dialogue.

Go to your spouse and schedule a time to sit down and deal with the conflict. Set the scheduled time to do this as soon as possible. Shulamith obviously wants to fix her conflict with Solomon as quickly as she can.

Choose a location in your house that is private, quiet, and neutral. Don't choose the bedroom or the special, cozy place you use for couple talk times and devotions. I usually recommend the kitchen or dining room table.

Step two: Pray

After you schedule your conflict discussion, each of you should go to a private place to calm down and pray for God's help in dealing with the conflict. Even a few minutes will help you simmer down from your peak of emotional intensity.

Step three: Focus on your spouse's positive qualities

Their focus on the positive is one of Solomon and Shulamith's secrets of working through a conflict. Before you sit down to talk, make yourself dwell on the favorable, attractive, and desirable things about your spouse. These things have not changed. Verbalize them to yourself and to God. This will take the edge off your anger and put you in a better frame of mind to successfully talk about the problem.

Step four: One at a time

When you are seated in your conflict-resolving location, one spouse should go first and share his or her feelings, thoughts, and point of view about the disagreement. This spouse is the Speaker, which makes the other spouse the Listener.

Communication must proceed one at a time. There will be one Speaker and one Listener at all times. There must be no interruptions whatever when a Speaker is talking; the Listener will get his or her turn and be afforded the same courtesy. If the Listener speaks during the Speaker's turn to talk, it is obvious that the Listener is not listening but thinking of what he will say and, therefore, no understanding is going on.

The Speaker, in a ten-minute maximum—or shorter—block of time, shares her opinion, feelings, and position, her "truth." The Listener's job is to say nothing at all during this time; his job is only to *listen* and *accept* and *understand*. When it is the Listener's turn to respond, he says nothing original, but only what will help the Speaker feel understood. He reflects, or feeds back just what the Speaker has said and indicates what she feels. "You're angry because I came home late and didn't call to let you know." "When I said _____, you are saying it made you feel _____."

You don't move on until the Speaker is satisfied that the Listener understands and the Speaker *feels* understood. Try to hold to the ten-minute rule. In dealing with a conflict, most often a spouse can actually sum up feelings, what is really bothering that person, in one statement. Doing this at the end of the ten minutes can be very helpful. What is essential is that the Speaker feels the spouse truly understands. When the Speaker tells the Listener she feels understood, *take a break* for a minimum of ten minutes. Let the understanding you just created settle in and take root.

After the break, return to your seats and *reverse the roles*. The Listener is now the Speaker. In ten minutes or fewer, he shares his point of view, his thoughts, his feelings, his truth. And, it's going to be different! You don't move on until the new Speaker feels understood by the Listener and says so.

You don't have to agree. In fact, you're not going to agree. But you do need to *acknowledge* and *accept*, unconditionally, the feelings of your spouse. ("I don't understand why you feel this way, but I accept your feelings and will act accordingly.") You do need to build understanding of your partner's feelings and position.

You may need some follow-up conversations in this stage. Sometimes, one time through is enough. Sometimes, it's not. If it's not, you need more one-at-a-time conversations.

It's common for the woman to need more processing to feel reassured that the man understands her. If she's unsettled and doesn't feel understood, the conflict can't be resolved. So, husband, let her keep talking, and work hard to communicate understanding to her. A few extra talks, with breaks between them, can make all the difference. That neither can refuse to have a session should be established as a rule.

Step five: Let's make a deal

Before you start this stage, take another break. This break should be for a few minutes to half a day or more. When both spouses are ready to resume, agree on a time and return one more time to your conflict resolution location.

If you must decide on some course of action or some behavior—a financial move, a parenting strategy, a schedule change, or something you want your partner to do or not do—you will need to work together to make a deal. With most of the anger gone and a substantial amount of understanding achieved, you will be in good shape to negotiate and reach an agreement. It is usually okay to go back and forth in this stage without staying in the Speaker-Listener roles. But if things begin to get too intense, go right back to those roles and the rules. This is like following the rules in a football game: without rules, there would be unfairness, chaos—and no fun.

The Deal must be specific and measurable. Don't be vague. Be willing to compromise. Sometimes, your spouse will agree to do it your way. Sometimes, you will agree to do it your spouse's way. Sometimes, you'll meet in the middle and work toward a compromise position. Every deal is reached on a trial basis. If it doesn't work, either partner can call a meeting to renegotiate.

Step six: Stop and start

When a conflict conversation gets off track, even a little, shut it down immediately. When something goes haywire, for example, when one of you reverts to your dysfunctional conflict style, you can't save that conversation. No couple can. It's over.

Either spouse can call for a stop, and it must be honored. Take a time out and get some space. It might be just five minutes. Go to the bathroom. Get a cup of coffee. Go to the backyard and do a primal scream. Tell your partner when you are ready to resume, and ask him or her to find you when he or she is ready. Then sit down, and start up where you left off.

Step seven: Make sure you make up

Okay, here's the fun part. You've worked hard to talk through the conflict. You deserve a reward. A treat. What activity can you think of that would be a special way to reconnect as a couple?

Sex! Makeup sex! It's some of the best, most passionate sex you'll ever have. You are relieved to be okay again as a couple. You're excited to be back on track in your love relationship. The sex is so terrific that it's almost worth it to get into a conflict on purpose. Almost.

If makeup sex is good enough for Solomon and Shulamith, it's good enough for us.

Clean Out Your Past, Unresolved Conflicts

Now that you know how to work through your current, present day conflicts, you need to clean out all the past, residual, unresolved conflicts that remain between you. This is very painful but necessary.

Expressing and forgiving resentments against others is God's truth (Eph. 4:15, 25–27; Col. 3:8–17; Matt. 5:23–24, 18:15–17, 21–35; Luke 17:3–4). We must forgive others, and the only way to do that is first to tell them directly the pain they have caused us.

In my clinical work with hundreds of married couples over the past twenty plus years, I have seen this truth of expression and forgiveness demonstrated over and over again. When spouses forgive each other for all hurts in the past, their love is renewed. Take the following steps, and you can experience the same renewal.

Step one: Write a letter

Sit down and write an absolutely honest letter to your spouse about the hurts and resentments you are harboring against him or her. Before you begin, pray that God will guide you in the writing. Pray that he will give you the memories and the emotions that must be expressed. Pray that he will enable you to truly forgive your spouse.

This letter will not be general. It will be as specific and detailed as you can make it. Re-create memories in vivid detail. Share your emotions completely and in all their intensity. It is a letter of truth. No sugarcoating or minimizing or rationalizing. If it's forty pages long, so be it. You are cleaning out every hurt and resentment that God brings to your memory. Do not—do not—attack the person in this letter. Make it an expression of your feelings only. Also, this does *not* include trivial matters that have never been significant to you.

As you write, pray that the Lord will give you the power to forgive. Use the language of forgiveness in your words. After expressing the truth, the details and emotions about an event, write these types of sentences: "I forgive you for this behavior. With God's help and power, I release the pain and resentment against you for what you did."

Step two: Read the letter to your spouse

Tell your spouse what you have written and why. Make it clear that the purpose of the letter is to forgive. Schedule a time to sit down in your home and read the letter to your spouse. If you have children, make sure they are not in the home during the reading.

As you sit down to read, pray with your spouse that God will be with you both and that he will use the truth in the letter to produce forgiveness. Ask your spouse to listen and not interrupt. Ask your spouse to believe your truth, simply accept your feelings, and not argue with them. Read the letter, no matter how long it takes.

Step three: Follow-up talks

After the reading, it is almost always necessary to have a series of follow-up conversations. In these conversations, you go over some of the material in the letter and ask your spouse to listen and reflect. You are clearing out any leftover pain and looking for reassurance that your spouse understands what happened and its impact on you.

In these follow-up talks, you both will use the Seven Steps of Conflict Resolution taught earlier in this chapter. Praying— as a couple—before each follow-up talk is a good idea. Ask your spouse to do his best to reflect (say back to you) what you are saying and your emotions. After you feel understood on a particular resentment, ask your spouse to gently and carefully present his feelings and point of view. He or she may disagree, but he or she must continue to believe your truth and validate your feelings about what happened.

These follow-up talks could begin immediately after the reading of the letter, but only if you both feel ready. Do not insist if you are hesitant or your spouse is hesitant. In most cases, I recommend letting the dust settle after the reading and scheduling the first follow up talk for the next day or so.

I urge you to go one at a time in this process of forgiveness of past hurts. In other words, the spouse who writes a letter first will be the focus until forgiveness has been achieved. This may take a few days to a few months, depending on how many hurts there are and how deep the hurts are. When one spouse feels finished and has forgiven, the other spouse can write his or her letter and begin the process of forgiveness.

This is a simple, brief description of what can be a very complicated, lengthy process. If either of you has or both of you have a pool of minor resentments, you'll be able to follow these steps on your own and be successful. But, if the pool of resentments includes deep, traumatic hurts (adultery, sexual addition, pornography, alcoholism, drug addiction, verbal abuse, physical abuse, chronic lying, etc.), you will need a Christian therapist to guide you through the process.

Ask your pastor for a referral or call Focus on the Family (1-800-A-FAMILY) and get a list of Christian therapists in your local area.

Conflict, while normal and inevitable, is a very, very difficult area of marriage. That's why God includes Solomon and Shulamith's story of conflict in the Song. Satan tries to use conflict to damage and destroy love but, as we have seen in the marriage of Solomon and Shulamith, God wants to use conflict to produce a renewed and passionate love.

16

Do You Want to Have Sex or Make Love?

Many of the couples I see in therapy wonder how to initiate successful sexual experiences. I'll bet you wonder too. What behaviors will create a mood conducive to sex? How do we navigate around schedules, jobs, chores, and kids, to end up in the bedroom? What do we do and say to create sexual interest and get us ready to engage in great sex?

I have good news. You've come to the right place. I think you'll find some effective, if somewhat shocking, answers to these important questions in the following scenarios.

The Front Door Diva

The husband walks slowly up to the front door of his home. It's been a long week. He's been late coming home five days in a row. To make matters worse, he hasn't called his dear wife on even one of these days to tell her he'd be late. They haven't communicated much, and he's been no help with the kids and the household chores. As he reaches for the doorknob, he assumes he'll get a frosty reception. "And frankly," he thinks to himself, "I wouldn't blame her."

He turns the doorknob and is surprised to find a sticky substance smeared all over it. He smells his hand and realizes it's honey! Baffled, he pushes open the door and sees a large note taped to the carpet. It reads, "That's right, it's honey. Why? Because you're my honey! Go to the kitchen." On his way to the kitchen, he notices that the house is dark and empty. He thinks, "I hope they haven't left me." After wiping his hand on a paper towel, he reads the note on the counter: "No, we haven't left you. Actually, the kids have left because I made them leave. They're with friends all night long. I'm in the bedroom. I think you know the way."

As he walks down the hallway, he reads a series of notes taped to the floor every three feet. "This Way, Hunk-a-Hunk of Burning Love." "Pleasure Palace Just Ahead." "No Shirt, No Shoes, No Clothes, No Problem." Finally, taped to the bedroom door is this note: "Please Hurry! I Can't Stand to Wait Any Longer!"

He opens the door and his heart skips a beat as he sees his wife, wearing a skimpy negligee, lounging on the bed. She purrs, "I know you've been working hard. Now, I want you to work on me. Take me, I'm yours."

The Very Late in the Day Don Juan

It's finally the end of the day, and the husband and wife are preparing to go to bed. It was a pretty good day. They both helped the kids with their homework, they ate dinner as a family, he took out the trash, she did a few loads of laundry, and they watched some television after the kids went to bed. She tried to start a few conversations, but he just mumbled some replies and didn't seem interested. It was their typical evening. Nothing horrible. Nothing spectacular. Just okay.

They wash their faces, brush their teeth, and perform other before-bed tasks. She puts on her special face cream. They crawl into bed, give each other a peck kiss, and turn out the light. She falls asleep almost immediately. End of story, right? Wrong.

He fidgets for about ten minutes, then shakes her and asks, "Are you awake?" "I am now," she answers. He says, "I can't get to sleep." She asks, "Is there anything I can do for you?" He replies, "Well, yes, there is. I'd like to have sex."

She immediately lights up and says, "Oh, what a relief! I was hoping all evening that you'd ask me. In fact, I was just having a bad dream in which a whole day went by and you didn't ask me for sex. Plus, you know how I love surprises! I know what's going to happen. You'll have an orgasm in five minutes, roll over, and go right to sleep. I won't have an orgasm and will be up for an hour before I can drop off. It's one of our marital traditions. Come over here, big boy, and let's help you get to sleep."

The Kitchen Casanova

It's six o'clock in the evening, and the wife is in full swing. She's making dinner, helping the kids with their homework, working on a load of laundry, and talking to a friend on the phone. Her husband got home about thirty minutes ago and, as is his custom, has been in their bedroom decompressing after his workday.

With no idea of what her day has been like or what her current state of mind is, he comes up behind her at the stove and starts rubbing her shoulders. "That feels good, honey," she sighs. He whispers in her ear, "I've got something that will make you feel even better. Let's go to the bedroom for a quickie before dinner."

She turns to face him and says, "You want sex now? Right now? I can't believe what I'm hearing! I ran the kids around all day, went to the grocery store twice, had to go to the post office because you forgot that package to my mother, and my period is about to start. And we haven't really had a decent conversation in two days. Not to mention, I'm kind of busy right now with dinner, laundry, and homework.

"What you're offering me is an escape from all this stress! Talking is overrated, anyway. Baby, you're a lifesaver! Let's do it! Last one to the bedroom is a rotten egg!"

She puts the food on simmer and says to the kids, "You're on your own with the homework. Finish it and pop in one of your movies. Mommy and Daddy need some alone time." With a skip in her step, she moves toward the bedroom and a wonderful oasis of stress release and love.

Let's Get a Grip on Reality

Can you picture these scenarios happening in your house? Honestly, can you? Of course not! I hate to break it to the husbands, but these stories are sheer fantasy. You husbands were thinking, "Oh, yeah! I can't believe Dr. Clarke is recommending these approaches to sex! This is my dream come true!" You wives were rolling your eyes and fighting a gag reflex.

The reality is, great sex happens only when you prepare for it. This is especially crucial for your wife to enjoy sex. Unlike the couples in these made up stories, you can't enjoy passionate, exciting sex on the spur of the moment. I wish you could! I wish *I* could!

I wish—without warning—I could grab my beautiful blonde, Sandy, throw her on the bed, and make wild, passionate love to her. I can't do that. If I tried, Sandy would be horrified. Disgusted. She'd probably call the police. And who could blame her?

If I want great sex with Sandy (and believe me, I do!), I need to prepare her for it. And Sandy needs to prepare me for it. When we both take the right steps, our sex is nothing less than terrific.

The Media Monster

All of us married couples have to fight and defeat a monster in order to successfully prepare for great sexual encounters. The monster is the media. Never underestimate the power of the media.

Satan is wise. He is very wise. He uses all the forms of media—magazines, newspapers, books, television, movies at home, movies in the theater, the Internet, radio—to fuel myths about sex. Satan's goal is to distort God's wonderful gift of sex and ruin it for us, and he's doing a bang-up job through the media. Very few married couples have the kind of beautiful, fulfilling, and exhilarating sex life that God has designed for marriage.

To help you beat the monster, I'm going to give you a good look at its lies. Here are the main media myths about sex and God's answering truths recorded in the Song.

Media's Myth: Sex outside Marriage Is a Great Idea

Sex outside marriage is glorified in the media. Big time. It's not merely an acceptable option. It is an expected and approved behavior. Anyone who chooses to remain a virgin until marriage is portrayed as hopeless, pathetic, and idiotic.

I mean, what kind of geeky, holier-than-thou prude waits until the wedding night to have sex for the first time? The media says you have to have intercourse before marriage in order to gain experience or to make sure you're sexually compatible. It's what the cool, hip, attractive singles do. Plus, it's natural and a lot of fun.

Once you're married, it's almost certain you'll have an affair or two. Or maybe even more. Sure, it's technically wrong, but who can resist? We all know marital passion doesn't last, so it's inevitable that you'll fall in love with someone new. Affairs are exciting and a real thrill ride. Just don't get caught. If you do get found out, get a divorce and move on to a new partner.

Funny, the media doesn't often share the grim statistics of sexually transmitted diseases, abortions, and broken relationships caused by sex outside of marriage, and the terrible trauma it causes the betrayed spouse and children. When those depressing numbers are reported, the basic message is: "This is just a part of life and there's nothing anyone can do about it." There is no indication given that all the pain and suffering can be avoided by sexual faithfulness in marriage.

The Song's truth: Sex belongs only inside marriage

Solomon and Shulamith wait until their wedding night to experience sexual activity and sexual intercourse for the first time. They are extremely physically attracted to each other, but they exercise self-control and patience in the physical part of their relationship.

Shulamith (2:7)
"I adjure you, O daughters of Jerusalem,
By the gazelles or by the hinds of the field,

That you will not arouse or awaken my love,
Until she pleases."

Here, Shulamith makes it clear that she intends to be patient with her physical desire for Solomon. She does not want to be fully aroused physically until the time is right. And that time, as we've already seen in the Song (5:1), is on her wedding night.

The best part of restricting intercourse to marriage is that God will bless your physical union richly. God makes a point of recording his blessing of the Song's lovers on their wedding night:

God (5:1b)
"Eat, friends;
Drink and imbibe deeply, O lovers."

If you have intercourse only inside your marriage, this same blessing can be yours. Solomon preached this same message over and over in the book of Proverbs (Prov. 2:16; 5:3; 7:5–20; 22:14; 23:27 are a few references) and in the book of Ecclesiastes (9:9), and it is the teaching of the whole Bible (1 Thess. 4:3–4). It must be important to God and therefore to us. Those who obey the Bible in this regard have the singular thrill of joyful memories created with this one person.

Media's Myth: Sex Is the Most Important Part of a Relationship

I'll go ahead and state the obvious: we live in a sex-drenched world. Most of the reports on the entertainment television shows concentrate on the sexual sins and immoral behavior of celebrities: television stars, movie stars, sports stars, musicians, and politicians.

Many television shows (sitcoms, dramas, soap operas) and movies focus on the sex lives of their characters. The characters talk about having sex, they have sex, they talk about the quality and quantity of their sex, and they continually find new partners with whom they can have sex. Literally, almost every show glamorizes not marital sex, but sex between *any* persons. With audacity, they proclaim the message that sex without marriage is a normal practice of life.

Television commercials offer little respite from the sexual bombardment. Reflecting on a current television commercial, if I have to see lingerie-clad models wearing those ridiculous wings one more time, I'll scream. No normal wife is going to parade into her bedroom wearing winged lingerie! If a wife did try to jump into bed with wings, her husband would feel as though he were making love to a giant moth.

The message media is screaming is: Sex is the foundation of every relationship. Nothing else really matters. Sex is everything.

The Song's truth: Sex is one of the many important parts of marriage

It's true that the Song has a lot to say about sex. It is portrayed, as it should be, as a very important part of a marriage. But, as we've seen in the previous chapters, the Song also showcases many other important parts of marriage: priority, positives, playfulness, pursuit, presence of God, and problem resolution.

The point is that marriage is a multifaceted relationship. Sex, while certainly critical, is not the foundation of the bond between a husband and a wife. *God, and the connection a couple shares in him* (5:1; 8:6–7), is the bedrock upon which all true marital love rests.

Media's Myth: Great Sex with One Partner Never Lasts

No one can continue to enjoy great sex with one partner over the long term. Media communicates this myth over and over through all the failed relationships, adulteries, and sex with multiple partners it describes in all its various outlets.

Affairs happen because you lose your sexual desire and passion for your current partner. It's really not your fault. It's really not your partner's fault. It's also fun and exciting to "fool around" (the world's term for extramarital sex, which itself degrades sex and its special nature). So why not? Media totally ignores and does not even hint at the consequences of this behavior. Whether you're married or not, you will have multiple sexual partners over the course of your lifetime. You'll have great—although temporary—sex with each of these partners.

The Song's truth: Great sex with one spouse can last a lifetime

The Song is the true story of a love that lasts a lifetime. Solomon and Shulamith's love does not end (8:6–7). Because the two lovers build their love God's way, it remains strong, vibrant, and passionate. In every aspect. Including sex.

In the Song, there is no premarital sex. There is no adultery. There is no loss of physical chemistry and passion. There is a *spiritual foundation*, a variety of *emotional connections*, and a never-ending stream of sexual energy and joy.

Media's Myth: Great Sex Never Requires Any Preparation

The only preparation needed for a great sexual experience is two naked bodies. A spiritual connection? Please! There is no God, and if by any slim chance there is, he isn't interested in sex. An emotional connection? Talk is overrated and just wastes time. When you feel the urge, just do it. Just have sex.

Great sex just happens. And it usually happens quickly. How many times have you seen a couple on television or in a movie—a couple who may have just met twenty minutes earlier—suddenly throw themselves at each other in a frenzy of passion? They literally rip each other's clothes off and go for it.

The Song's truth: Great sex always requires preparation

Solomon and Shulamith would laugh their heads off at the twenty-first-century media's presentation of sex without preparation. They know better. Following God's design and guidance, Solomon and Shulamith carefully prepare for their sexual experiences.

Their sex is beyond great. It is better than any sex the media holds up as an example of how to connect physically. Solomon and Shulamith come together regularly in specific spiritual, emotional, and physical ways other than intercourse. As they meet each other's deepest needs, great sex is their reward. The best part is that how they do it has been revealed by God. It's all in the Song.

17

How to Have a Sensuous Wife

Solomon and Shulamith have an amazing sex life. It is passionate. It is incredibly intimate. It is fulfilling. It is loads of fun. It is intensely pleasurable. It is a beautiful, *physical* expression of their always growing *spiritual* and *emotional* love for each other.

Best of all, their fantastic sex is real. Solomon and Shulamith's sexual relationship is worlds apart from the fantasy world of the media. They're not actors. They're not pretending. They're not following a script. They are a real couple having a wonderful time having real sex.

The question is: what are Solomon and Shulamith's secrets to their sensuous marriage? The answer is: *they prepare for great sex by meeting each other's deepest needs.*

It's true that all the passion principles Solomon and Shulamith practice in their relationship play a part in preparing them for physical intimacy. But there are two particular needs that *specifically* prepare these lovers for the bedroom.

Solomon consistently meets one critically important need in Shulamith's life. Shulamith consistently meets one critically important need in Solomon's life. When they both do their jobs and meet these needs, they are ready to hit the bedroom with a beautiful bang. When you and your lover follow their example, your sex will take off too.

First, in this chapter I explain how Solomon meets Shulamith's need. Then, in the following chapter I explain how Shulamith meets Solomon's need.

Husband, Meet Her Need for Emotional Intimacy

Husband, it's your job to meet your wife's need for emotional intimacy. It's one of her deepest needs. It's why she married you! As a means to this, she longs to connect verbally with you. To be close to you. To know you. To share your life.

Let's say we give your wife the choice between an intimate, deep conversation with you or sex with you. Which will she choose? We both know she'll choose the deep conversation. And, if she gets the deep conversation, that's preparation for sex. Keep that in mind.

What Every Woman Needs

Husband, your job is to love your dear wife. I'm sure you do love her, *but it doesn't count unless she feels loved.* There is no way she'll feel loved if you don't meet her need for emotional intimacy. It's how God made her. *It's every woman's main love language.*

Shulamith (2:3b)

> "In his shade I took great delight and sat down,
> And his fruit was sweet to my taste."

Shulamith loves to be alone with Solomon and to hear him talk. "Fruit" here refers to his speech. What is her reaction when Solomon speaks to her?

Shulamith (2:5–6)

> "Sustain me with raisin cakes,
> Refresh me with apples,
> Because I am lovesick.
> Let his left hand be under my head
> And his right hand embrace me."

See what a little personal talking does to her? She's overcome with the intensity of her feelings of love for Solomon. She is drawn to him physically. She wants him to kiss her and caress her body.

The same progression of male speech and female physical desire is recorded a few chapters later.

Shulamith (5:16)

> "His mouth is full of sweetness.
> And he is wholly desirable."

It's like a magic potion! When she hears him talk to her, her physical desire for him is ignited. She doesn't find him sort of desirable. She finds him "wholly" desirable. She wants him in bed.

Solomon is no fool. He knows that there are two elements in meeting Shulamith's need for emotional intimacy. The first is sharing personally with her. The second is *listening attentively* to her when she speaks.

Solomon (2:14)

"Let me hear your voice;

For your voice is sweet."

Is this guy a relationship genius or what? He asks her to talk. He loves to hear her talk. He hangs on her every word.

Mister Avoidance

The problem is, husband, you are a master at avoiding emotional intimacy. It's what you do! You will automatically do whatever it takes to weasel out of a close, deep conversation with your wife. Won't you?

One of your classic escape lines is, "I don't know." How many times has your poor wife heard that? I can guarantee you it's getting old. These three little words are a thing of beauty. They work like a charm. They kill a conversation cold.

She asks, "How was your day?"

He says, "I don't know."

She asks, "How are you doing?"

He says, "I don't know."

She asks, "How do you feel about that?"

He says, "I don't know."

She asks, "What do you think about that decision we have to make?"

He says, "I don't know."

You're telling your wife, "I wish I could talk, honey, but there's nothing in my head. Nothing." Is it a form of amnesia? Or brain damage? No. It's just avoidance of emotional intimacy.

As part of one of my marriage seminars, I say to the wives: "Ladies, it's high time you give him some of his own medicine. I'm going to ask some questions as if I'm your husband. After each question, I want you to say, out loud, "I don't know."

He asks, "What are we having for dinner?"
You say, "I don't know."
He asks, "Where are my socks?"
You say, "I don't know."
He asks, "When are you going to wash my underwear?"
You say, "I don't know."
He asks, "Would you like to have sex?"
You say, "I don't know."

Believe me, the wives enjoy this little exercise immensely. Of course, husband, you have many other avoidance tricks you can use:

"I don't want to talk about it." You simply unilaterally decide to take that topic from the agenda.

"This isn't a good time to talk." You indicate there's going to be a good time real soon. Sure!

"I'm too busy." Busy, busy, busy. You communicate that if you weren't so busy, you'd love to talk about that topic that you really don't want to talk about.

"Fine," "Okay," and "Pretty good." These massive generalizations in answer to questions she asks you, tell her . . . nothing, which is your point in saying them.

"Doc, Why Isn't She into Sex?"

Hundreds of husbands have complained to me that their wives aren't interested in sex. They tell me: "Doc, my wife doesn't want to be with me sexually. She'll say no when I ask, or come up with some lame excuse. She's avoiding me! When she does agree to sex, I can tell it's just another chore for her. What can I do to get her more interested?"

I give all these husbands the same response: "I've talked to your wife. A major problem is that you're not meeting her need for emotional intimacy. You can't just pursue her physically and expect her to respond. When you consistently meet her need for emotional intimacy, four wonderful things happen: she'll feel closer to you, she'll be drawn to you physically, she'll respond to you in bed, and she'll even pursue you sexually."

Follow Solomon's Example

God has given us husbands an example to follow to achieve this goal we all desire to reach. Wouldn't the wisest man who ever lived (1 Kings 3:12) know how to meet a woman's central need? You better believe he would. Solomon makes his wife, Shulamith, feel loved, and he does it by meeting her need for emotional intimacy.

In the Song, who does more of the initiating in emotional intimacy? Solomon! He does this because it makes Shulamith feel loved and because he enjoys being close to her emotionally. A secondary benefit is that Shulamith is warm, soft, complimentary, and all over him physically. Every man's dream!

Read chapter four in the Song, and you'll see a master at work. In 4:1–10, Solomon describes the beauty of Shulamith's body and character. He is talking personally. He is being vulnerable. He is expressing his deep love for his woman. He is meeting her need for emotional intimacy.

In 4:11, the real fun begins. Because Solomon touches Shulamith's heart and creates an *emotional bond*, now the *physical bond* can occur. The two lovers kiss passionately, get involved in some serious foreplay, and have intercourse.

In 4:15, Shulamith is aroused. In 4:16, her sexual response reaches a peak. She is totally into the sexual experience. She is not counting cracks in the ceiling. She's not thinking about the chores she still has to do when sex is over. She's not doing mental gymnastics to endure intercourse.

No way! Shulamith is enjoying every second of this sexual encounter with Solomon. She is fully engaged. She is very, very responsive. Why is Shulamith so into sex? She loves sex and responds to Solomon passionately because *first* he talks to her. He listens to her. He connects to her *emotionally*.

Talk Times and Spiritual Bonding

You're thinking, "Okay, Doc, you've convinced me. Emotional connection comes before physical connection. But, how do I connect emotionally with my wife? How do I consistently meet her need for emotional intimacy?"

The two essential keys to creating an ongoing emotional connection with your wife are: couple talk times and spiritual bonding. Read chapter four in this book again, this time with your wife. And, start having four thirty-minute couple talk times per week. Follow the progressive steps in your talk times: (1) start with a brief prayer, (2) read your couple's devotional, (3) discuss what's on your mind, (4) pray together, and (5) move from prayer to conversation.

Go back and reread chapter twelve again with your wife, and start a spiritual bonding process. Follow the four passion principles: (1) come to Christ, (2) share your personal spiritual growth, (3) pray together, and (4) read the Bible together. *God* will give you the ability to open up and share personally with your wife.

Practice, practice, practice. You'll get better and better at emotionally and spiritually connecting with your wife. Your reward will be a much more intimate marriage and a much more exciting sex life.

I guess you've noticed, husband, that I addressed you first in this meeting-the-critical-need-of-your-spouse process. That was no accident. It has been my personal and professional experience that it is vital for the husband to go first and meet his wife's need for emotional intimacy. With her need met, the wife feels safe and confident in her husband's love and can then meet his need.

18

How to Have a Sensitive Husband

What is the one critically important need in a husband's life that a wife must meet? I'll bet you wives are wracking your brains right now. "Wow! There are so many possibilities! What could my husband's main need be?"

Coffee in the morning?
Clean underwear and socks?
Complete command of the television remote control?
A well-stocked refrigerator?
A steak dinner once a week?
Never being asked to go to the ballet or the opera?

While all these needs are important, none reach the level of critical. It's a real puzzler, isn't it? Let me end the suspense.

I realize you're dying to know what your husband really needs from you. Get ready for the shock of your life.

Wife, Meet His Need for Physical Intimacy

Wife, it's your job to meet your husband's need for physical intimacy. I doubt that you're stunned to hear this. You knew this was coming, didn't you?

Being physically close to you, through making out and especially sexual closeness and intercourse, is one of your husband's deepest needs. When his need for physical intimacy is met, he feels close to you. He feels in love with you. He feels confident. He feels like a man.

His need for regular, passionate touch and intercourse is hard-wired into him. Wife, you have no idea the huge influence your husband's sex drive has on his life. His desire to have sex with you is beyond strong. If scientists were to do tests comparing the power of nuclear chain reactions and testosterone, the nuclear chain reactions would come in second. Engaging in regular sexual relations with you is directly connected to his mental health. His emotional well-being depends on the quantity and quality of his sex with you.

What Every Man Needs

Closely allied to his need for physical intimacy is his need for respect from you. There is no way he'll feel respected if you don't meet his need for physical intimacy. *It's every man's main love language.*

Solomon clearly expresses his deep need for physical intimacy with Shulamith. Ten times in the Song, he calls her *beautiful.* He is very attracted to her and has a powerful desire to be with her physically.

Solomon spends a considerable amount of time giving Shulamith vivid, detailed descriptions of her lovely body (4:1–7, 15; 7:1–8). He revels in her beauty and loves to touch and caress all the parts of her marvelous body. He needs her body and isn't ashamed to let her know. He needs to be sexually intimate with her. He needs to be physically one with her.

Mrs. Avoidance

The problem is, wife, that you can be a master at avoiding physical intimacy. Here's a list of your lame excuses to sidestep sex with my comments added. This is not to deny that sometimes there are legitimate reasons for you to turn down sex. Husbands, though it may be tough, should accept these reasons with understanding.

Wife: "I don't have time, honey."

Dave Clarke: "You always have time for what's important. Sex isn't going to take three hours!"

Wife: "I've got to finish my chores, honey."

Dave Clarke: "You've just told your husband that the laundry, cleaning the toilets, and doing the dishes are more important than he is. That's not showing him respect. That's an insult. Do the chores, with his help, after sex."

Wife: "I'm too tired, honey."

Dave Clarke: "I'll buy that if you're ninety years old. Or, if you've just completed a triathlon."

Wife: "I've got to meet the kids' needs, honey."

Dave Clarke: "Oh, no you don't! Not before meeting his needs. You've forgotten that your husband is above the kids on your priority list. If anyone waits, it ought to be the kids."

Wife: "I have a headache, honey."

Dave Clarke: "Ahhh, one of the all-time classic lines! Baby, your headache better be a real doozy. He needs to see you taking big horse pills for it. Unless it's a migraine, the pills will take it away in about twenty minutes. Then— guess what?—you can have sex with no ill effects."

Wife: "It's too close to my period, honey."

Dave Clarke: "But it isn't your period yet, right? PMS is real, but it shouldn't always prevent physical intimacy. Maybe you can't have intercourse, but you can still be intimate."

Wife: "We just had sex a few days ago, honey!"

Dave Clarke: "Number one: you're probably wrong. Women remember everything except the last time they had sex. I'll bet it was more like seven days ago. Number two: so what if it was a few days ago? For a man, a few days is an eternity."

Do these excuses sound familiar, men? Getting old, aren't they?

Wife, you're also too passive, sexually. You almost always make him do the asking. This automatically puts you in a defensive position. Agreeing to sex is a lot different from desiring sex. Your husband desperately needs you to *want* him sexually.

Too many wives see sex as just another chore. "Feed the dog, wipe the kitchen counter, have sex with Bob." Or, they see it as a "wifely duty." If this is your attitude, don't bother having sex at all. You're stripping away his manhood and humiliating him.

Wife, that guy sitting on your couch in the raggedy gym shorts and chili-stained T-shirt is your man. He's the only man you have! He needs—in addition to his obvious need for some new casual clothes—your physical touch.

Follow Shulamith's Example

Wife, the answer is to stop avoiding him and start pursuing him sexually. If he's working to meet your need for emotional intimacy, then stop resisting him sexually or showing him little or no interest in sex. Stop being only a responder. Pursue him! Go after him sexually!

This isn't my idea, even though I like it. It's God's idea. Your biblical example is Shulamith, Solomon's wife. She knows exactly what she is doing in the physical area of her marriage. She makes Solomon feel respected. One of the main ways she does it is by pursuing him physically.

Shulamith talks to Solomon about being physically intimate with him (1:2–4, 16; 2:6, 17; 7:10–13; 8:1–3, 14). But she is not a tease. She actively participates in a full range of sexual activities with him. She kisses him (4:11; 5:13; 7:8–9). She makes out with him (2:6). She has intercourse with him (4:16–5:1; 7:1–9, 10–13).

At the very beginning of the Song, God chooses to showcase the sexual assertiveness of Shulamith. Read her words and picture *yourself* saying them:

Shulamith (1:2–4a)
"May he kiss me with the kisses of his mouth!
For your love is better than wine.
Your oils have a pleasing fragrance,
Your name is like purified oil;

Therefore the maidens love you.

Draw me after you and let us run together!

The king has brought me into his chambers . . ."

She is coming on to Solomon! She wants to be kissed. She wants to make love to him. She praises his character and his superb lovemaking ability. She knows her sexual pursuit of him meets one of his most significant needs. She obviously enjoys chasing—and catching—Solomon.

Shulamith is not a reluctant sexual partner. She isn't making him pursue her. She's not avoiding him. She's not playing hard to get. She is going after him physically. Her desire is real. She wants him!

Shulamith doesn't stop at kissing Solomon and talking about making love with him. In chapters four and seven, she makes out as part of pre-intercourse foreplay. She also talks about making out without intercourse:

Shulamith (2:6)

"Let his left hand be under my head
And his right hand embrace me."

Here, she wants Solomon to be intimate with her but not necessarily complete the entire sexual act. She knows there is a lot of fun and erotic touching they can do without having intercourse.

The one time in the Song that Shulamith denies Solomon sex (5:2–8), she immediately regrets it and goes searching for him! When was the last time that happened in your home?

In the Song, who does more of the initiating in physical intimacy? Shulamith! Surprised? Shulamith pursues

Solomon physically *more* than *he* pursues *her*. What does Shulamith get in return for all her physical pursuit? She gets a man who is gentle, kind, attentive, and working at connecting with her emotionally. She gets every woman's dream!

In 2:14, a verse we've looked at before, Solomon has made time to be alone with Shulamith. He is listening to her. He's totally focused on her. He is one hundred percent sensitive. He wants to know her. All of her.

Wife, do you want your husband to treat you like this? I know you do. All right, then. I want you to pursue your husband physically in the following three ways.

Be Honest with Him

Tell him, gently but firmly, what you need to be more interested in sex. Teamwork with the kids and chores. Romance. More conversations. A deeper level of ongoing emotional intimacy. Spiritual bonding. Be clear that while you'll do your best to pursue him, there are specific actions he can take which will help motivate you.

In a neutral and non-bedroom setting, tell him what turns you off sexually and what turns you on. Be specific. As Shulamith did, tell him exactly how you want him to touch you in the bedroom.

Tell him about the pain in your past that's blocking you sexually. It could be family of origin pain. Father pain. Old boyfriend pain. Ex-spouse pain. Resentments against him. When you talk this pain out with him, you can heal together. If your husband is blocked sexually, if past unhappy experiences with sex are interfering with his pleasure, he has to tell you about his past pain also.

Schedule Sex

Sit down with your husband every weekend and schedule your times of intercourse. Life is very busy, and if you don't schedule sex, it won't happen as often as it should.

Many married couples crab to me: "Oh, but setting specific times will destroy our spontaneity." My response is, "First, you've been trying to have spontaneous sex ever since your honeymoon. How is that going? Second, a lack of spontaneity is a lot better than a lack of sex. Third, you can generate all the spontaneity and creativity you want once you are in the bedroom."

And if you have children, you can kiss your spontaneity goodbye. But parenthood does not mean you have to kiss your sex goodbye. What you have to do is kiss your children goodbye as you leave them to go have sex in your bedroom. Children are not mentioned in the Song! Why? Because the absence of children is required for the existence of romantic passion and sex. Keep your bedroom locked and make it known that you are not be to be bothered for the next forty-five minutes.

By the way, don't worry about your teenagers knocking on your love nest door. If your teens think you may be having sex in there, they'll act as if you have Bubonic Plague. They'll scurry away to the farthest corner of the house and crank up their music.

I know what you're thinking, wife. "I can't have sex if my kids are awake. It could scar them for life." I say, "It'll scar your husband and your marriage for life if you allow your children to dictate when you engage in intercourse. It's not always about them! So, get over your resistance and reclaim your sexual freedom!"

If you have to say no to your husband's request for intercourse, make it a qualified and temporary no. Immediately after saying no, schedule a time when you can have intercourse. Your husband needs some hope to know you're not rejecting him.

Be Sexually Assertive

Kiss him spontaneously. Like you mean it. Lingering and multiple kisses. Touch him often in affectionate, sexual ways. Massage his neck. His back. His scalp. His feet. Make sure these are real, heartfelt massages. Don't bother with any more of those pitiful, wimpy massages. Nothing says, "I could care less" better than a pathetic, halfhearted, five-minute massage. A ten- to fifteen-minute massage says, "I love you and respect you, stud!" He'll be putty in your hands.

Make out touching is a lost art in marriage. Most couples make out only in order to prepare for intercourse. That's not enough making out during the week! Initiate make out sessions. Heavy petting. You know what I mean—the kind of serious touching, caressing, and kissing that lovers around the world do on a regular basis. You *are* lovers, aren't you? I'm not talking about intercourse. Make it clear up front to your husband that this will be non-intercourse touching. However, it can be everything *but* intercourse. This kind of make out touching keeps the two of you close, connected, stress-free, and prepares you for your scheduled times of intercourse.

Initiate intercourse. Ask him for it. Schedule it with him. Be responsive in bed. Let yourself go! Shulamith does, and she enjoys the sexual experience every bit as much as Solomon does.

19

Stop Making the Same Old Mistakes in the Bedroom

I can sense your excitement. Your keen anticipation. We've finally arrived in the bedroom. The men are thinking: "What took you so long?" All you men who have skipped ahead need to go back and read the previous eighteen chapters. The Song's passion principles we've learned so far are designed to create intimacy, energize your passion, and get you ready for the bedroom.

I just told Sandy that I was about to start the two chapters on sex. She raised her eyebrow, cocked her beautiful, blonde head the way she does, and said, "Really? Two chapters? I'd be surprised if you can come up with two pages of material."

The truth is, I don't have to be an expert to provide you with world-class, state of the art instruction about sex. Don't get me wrong. I do know something about sex. Sandy and I have been married for twenty-five years. In addition to a lot of years of training, I've also talked to hundreds of married couples in my office about their sexual problems.

So, these experiences will help me help you. But the main source of wisdom about sex in these chapters will be the Song. You'd kind of expect the greatest love poem of all time to contain some insightful guidance in the area of sex. You'd be right.

As I've done for every other passion principle, I will initially describe what married couples do wrong and then present the teaching of the Song. In this chapter, I'll cover the top seven sexual mistakes made by most married couples. In the next chapter, I'll teach the Song's solutions to these mistakes.

Mistake #1: Lack of Atmosphere in the Bedroom

The woman's physical arousal and enjoyment is directly connected to the atmosphere of the place she's having sex. She will be aware—and affected by—every detail of her surroundings.

The wife has all kinds of questions running through her head as she enters the bedroom: "Is it quiet? Is it private? Is it secure? Is it clean? Is it tidy? Does it smell nice? Is it warm and romantic? Is the lighting right? Does the bed look good? Are the bed sheets clean?"

The husband has one thing in his head as he enters the bedroom: "We're gonna have sex!" Simple, almost pathetic, but true.

See the potential for problems here? I think the following dialogue will shed more light on the matter.

Husband: "Doc, I need help. My wife doesn't enjoy having sex with me. She'll do it, but her heart is not in it. She seems tense and distracted when we're in the bedroom anticipating sex."

Dave Clarke: "Describe the bedroom."

Husband: "Our bedroom? Who cares about our bedroom?"

Dave Clarke: "Your wife does. Humor me. Answer these questions. First, what type of door does your bedroom have?"

Husband: "It's one of those plywood doors."

Dave Clarke: "What kind of lock does the door have?"

Husband: "It's got one of those push-button locks, but I'm not sure the thing even works."

Dave Clarke: "What's on the floor?"

Husband: "At the foot of the bed there is a pile of my semi-dirty clothes. I also keep my tennis shoes by the pile. (Defensively:) But you can't see the clothes or the shoes from the bed."

Dave Clarke: "Tell me about the closet."

Husband (beginning to squirm): "Well, my side is a little messy. I just kind of toss my work shoes in front of it and my casual shirts are stacked in clumps on the shelves. Oh, my wife has asked me for the past two years to fix the closet doors, but I haven't gotten around to it."

Dave Clarke: "Until you get around to it, I wouldn't expect your wife to get around to enjoying sex with you. Let's continue. Describe the lighting in your bedroom, especially during sex."

Husband (hanging his head): "Our overhead light has been broken for a year. We use the bathroom light, but it's still really too dark when we're trying to have sex."

Dave Clarke: "'Trying' is the right word. Making love by the bathroom light sounds very romantic. Maybe you could each wear one of those miner's hats with the light attached to the front. Now, tell me what your bed looks like."

Husband: "The mattress is old and lumpy. Yes, she's asked for a new one, but I hate to spend the money. The bedspread is ancient and has a bunch of holes and worn patches in it."

Dave Clarke: "I can't imagine why your wife doesn't enjoy sex with you. The door is paper-thin and may not even lock. Your dirty clothes and tennis shoes are on the floor. Your side of the closet is a mess, and you won't fix the closet doors so your mess could at least be hidden. Your bedroom has the lighting of a cave. Your wife can look up from this bed of burning passion during sex and see the broken light you haven't fixed. Your mattress is a medieval torture rack. The bedspread was fine when Cleopatra used it, but now it is worn out and shabby."

The poor husband wasn't off the hook yet. After some more questioning, I found out he was not careful in preparing his body for sex. He didn't always take a shower. He didn't always use deodorant or cologne. He didn't always shave! He didn't always brush his teeth!

I told him he was lucky his wife had sex with him at all. I told him—and I was serious—to give his long-suffering wife a large trophy bearing this inscription: "Thank You for All the Times You've Had Sex with a Slob like Me."

Mistake #2: Making Love Only in the Bedroom

I had just completed a Friday evening talk on romance and sex at a resort hotel. It was the first session of a Marriage Retreat hosted by a church. As I usually do, I told the couples that I expected them to go to their rooms to practice the sexual principles I had just covered. I told them not to feel sorry for me because Sandy wasn't able to make the trip with me.

The next morning, between sessions, a couple came up to me and sheepishly admitted that they had not had sex the night before. I asked, "Why not?" The husband said, "We decided to watch a football game instead." The wife also seemed to be okay with this choice of entertainment.

I asked them, "Are you crazy? You're here at a beautiful hotel, on a Marriage Retreat, without your kids, you heard a juicy, very helpful, practical talk on sex, and you don't have sex? What I'm going to do is call the front desk, report you, and have you immediately kicked out of the hotel. I'll give your lovely room to a married couple who will make better use of it. You can sleep in the car tonight."

Mistake #3: It's Too Quiet

After decades of research, I have discovered the quietest place in the world. The answer may surprise you. Is it a library? A church? The middle of a massive pine forest? A monastery after evening prayers? A crystal blue lake in the Arctic Refuge? No. None of these places earned the top spot. The quietest place in the world is the bedroom of the average married couple during sex.

Actually, there is one place that is a close second. A cemetery. Like a cemetery, the marital bedroom during sex is extremely quiet and shows very few signs of life. Many married couples—too many—seem to think talking will disrupt the sexual experience. Wrong. Talking will greatly enhance the sexual experience.

When I see married couples who are struggling with sexual issues, I ask them to tell me what happens during foreplay. It's a tad awkward for them, but hey, that's therapy. Ninety-nine point nine percent report very little talking.

Dave Clarke: "Do you say any words at all?"

Husband: "Very few. I usually say, 'I'm ready now' just before intercourse."

Dave Clarke: "Why don't you ask her if *she's* ready?'

Wife: "We just don't do it that way."

Dave Clarke: "How do you know she's sufficiently aroused and close to orgasm if you don't ask her or she doesn't tell you? Without words, how can you fully express love? How can you tell your partner how and where you want to be touched? Without words, how can your sexual needs be met?"

Husband: "We don't talk and make love at the same time. I don't know why. We've always done it in silence. Other than grunts and groans."

Dave Clarke: "We have some work to do, because you can't truly experience the maximum pleasure of making love unless you talk during the experience."

Mistake #4: The Husband Is Way Too Fast

Men have won international fame, respect, and big money by setting speed records in a wide range of sports and other activities: running, swimming, auto racing, eating, cycling, skiing, boating, mountain climbing, hot air ballooning, flying. . . . Most of the time, speed is a wonderful achievement. It is admired and highly valued. But there is one area in which speed is not a good idea. That place is the bedroom.

The other night, Sandy and I were watching television. A commercial came on in which a man was asking his wife for sex. He said, "We have thirty minutes before the kids will get home, if you know what I mean." She replied, "Great, but what will we do with the other twenty-five minutes?"

I laughed out loud, but this situation really isn't funny. I've talked to hundreds of wives who have shared with me their terrible frustration with their husbands' speed. "It's all about him and when he's ready. That doesn't take long. I have zero chance to get aroused, and the experience ends up being painful and anticlimactic."

Mistake #5: The Wife Is Not Responsive

It seems to me that you wives get the short end of the stick in a number of areas. Childbirth, for starters. After nine months of carrying the child and undergoing huge changes in your body, the baby comes out one of two ways: the horribly painful birth canal/vaginal delivery, or your stomach being sliced open in a C-section.

You have to endure PMS every month, with its hormone-fueled mood shifts, irritability, and often uncomfortable physical symptoms. Following PMS, of course, is the monthly burden of blood flowing from your most sensitive body part.

In addition, you typically have too many jobs and not enough hours in the day to complete them. Laundry, cooking, cleaning, grocery shopping, kids' homework, school issues, church responsibilities, caring for your parents. . . . If you have another job outside the home, you get to come home and begin your second job of meeting the never-ending needs of your husband and children. Your work is truly never done.

Wouldn't it be fair, then, for wives to have an easier time experiencing sexual pleasure and achieving orgasm? Yes, it would be. But, it would not be reality in most cases. For a variety of reasons (some of which are in the previous paragraph) most wives struggle with letting go of their inhibitions and getting lost in the wonder of lovemaking.

Instead of letting yourself relax and giving yourself to your husband completely, you get tense. Preoccupied. Easily distracted. Your mind is on the jobs you haven't finished yet. You're tired. Weary. Your walls are up. Instead of experiencing the intense pleasure and stress releasing power of orgasm for *you*, you see sex as another service you perform for your husband.

You're not having much fun in sex. Your husband knows you're not having much fun, so he doesn't have much fun, either. It's time for the fun to begin.

Mistake #6: God Is Not Invited

When I think of all the married couples I've talked to about sex, only a handful have ever mentioned God as a part of their physical intimacy. Most couples don't see God as having any connection to their sexual lives.

We know God created sex. It is all his idea, his gift. And we know he wants us to enjoy it. That is immediately discerned by the fact that he tells us through the apostle Paul that we should *not deprive one another of it* (1 Cor. 7:5). We have not been given this gift only for procreation, only for the times we want to conceive children. Yet, incredibly, we're pretty sure he turns his back when we are doing it. We think it's weird to think of God being right there with us. Very sad, and very seriously mistaken thinking, but true. (This might be a carryover from past experiences when you engaged in sex surreptitiously or felt guilt when you did. These past bad memories must be dealt with and defused.)

So, we think we are on our own in the bedroom (or wherever we're having sex). God's not too interested in what we do sexually, and we don't want him there, anyway. All we can do is follow basic relationship principles and do our best. If we build a strong emotional bond, create a foundation of spiritual intimacy, and practice sexual techniques, we are fully convinced we'll be fine in the sexual area.

We might be "fine," but we won't be fabulous. Though God made us distinctly physical, mental, emotional, and spiritual, our sex experiences will be severely limited to *one* aspect of our beings: the physical. If we leave God out of the bedroom, we will never taste the full pleasure and meaning of sex.

Mistake #7: Nobody Hangs Around

I'm curious if you recognize this scene. A married couple is making love in their bedroom. They've been able to carve out forty minutes. Their kids are out of their hair. It's private. And quiet. They've enjoyed about thirty minutes of foreplay and both are reaching a peak of arousal. It's really going well! Intercourse takes place, and both are able to orgasm. Satisfaction. Pleasure. A great time together.

Immediately following their orgasms, they leave the bed. The husband bolts downstairs to turn on the ballgame and check his email. The wife takes a shower, checks the kids, and starts a load of laundry.

Can you see what's wrong with this picture? They started well. They had a very good sexual experience. But they did not finish well. Their lovemaking ended with a thud. They missed getting the most out of their sexual passion. The husband also *disregarded* a vital component of sex for his wife: not only is her arousal period almost always considerably longer than his, also unlike him, the "afterglow" for her is *slow, gradual*. To walk out on her prematurely leaves her unfulfilled, and he misses something special too.

Celebrating important achievements and basking in the afterglow is a key element in squeezing every ounce of pleasure and significance from life. When mountain climbers scale the mighty Everest, do they immediately start their descent? No! When a basketball player hits the winning shot at the final buzzer, does he or she calmly walk off the court? No! When God answers a critical prayer request and comes through for you, do you say a brief "thank you" and move on?

You know what everyone does—or ought to do—after something special happens. Celebrate! *Talk* about the accomplishment! Relive it! Share personal reflections and get the reactions of the others involved in what happened! Sex is no different. It needs to be celebrated.

20

Solomon and Shulamith's Spectacular Sex

That's right. You read that correctly. Spectacular! Solomon and Shulamith enjoy a sex life that is nothing short of amazing. Sadly, their sexual success is something most married couples never achieve. And that is not what God wants. God has planned and made available what Solomon and Shulamith have. That's why the story of their relationship, including details of their lovemaking, is in the Bible.

Solomon and Shulamith have seven secrets to success in sex. The Song's solutions to the top seven sexual mistakes will give you the ability to make love as you've never made love before.

Solution #1: Build a Love Nest

Solomon and Shulamith make love in a completely private and secure environment. There is no mention of anyone bothering them. Of course, who would have dared disturb the king and his wife? When they are alone in their bedroom, it is off limits to everyone.

You need to make sure your bedroom is as secure as Fort Knox. When you're in there together to make love, you are in the vault. Nobody leaves—hopefully—and nobody enters. Tell the peasants (your kids) not to bother the King and the Queen (you two).

Buy a solid and sturdy door that blocks much of the noise from either side. This kind of door is good for soundproofing but also adds to the aura of security. Put a dead bolt on the door if that is needed to protect you from disturbances. I'm not kidding. You want to know that no one can enter your bedroom during your most intimate times together. Unless your kids call the fire department and the firemen hack your door down with axes, no one is getting in.

The Song does not specifically describe the lovers' bedroom, but it's safe to assume that it is a very romantic setting. We know Solomon is a romantic man who praises Shulamith's beauty and character in great detail. He knows how to meet her needs and prepare her for sex. He certainly is aware of how important the atmosphere of the bedroom is to his wife.

I believe Solomon makes sure their bedroom is a beautiful and romantic place. He knows the mood is a vital, contributing factor to the experience. I can't picture Solomon saying to Shulamith: "Hey, honey, let's go into the bedroom and make love. Wow, sorry this place is such a mess! I told those servants to tidy up, make the bed, and put mints on the pillows. I'll just throw these sandals and robes into the closet and we can get on with it."

In that day, there was no electricity, so every room was lit with candles. So, Solomon and Shulamith are likely making love in candlelight. It's another great idea, because everybody looks better in candlelight! The flickering flames cast a soft, romantic glow in the bedroom. (This is why romantic restaurants use candles. You can't read the menu, but it isn't just about the food.)

Prepare your bedroom for the experience. Clean it up. Make the bed. Get shoes and clothes out of sight. Use a beautiful bedspread that your wife picks out. And use no electricity. Take a tip from the Song's lovers and get out the candles. You're not having sex in the city dump. You're making love in a gorgeous, romantic boudoir.

Solomon and Shulamith prepare their bodies for their sexual encounter too. What sense would it make for them to be stinky and nasty in a beautiful, romantic bedroom?

Shulamith (1:3a)

"Your oils have a pleasing fragrance . . ."

It was common in that day to oil your body in preparation for a special occasion. Sex certainly is a special occasion. Shulamith is saying she finds the scent of Solomon's perfumed oils erotic. Are you getting this, husbands? Your smelly armpits will turn her off. Your clean, scented body will turn her on. Any questions?

Shulamith uses the power of smell to get Solomon's motor running.

Solomon (4:11b)

"And the fragrance of your garments is like the fragrance of Lebanon."

Translation: "You are smelling very, very good to me, baby!" Shulamith uses fragrance to enhance her sexual appeal and get Solomon's attention. She succeeds.

Without fail, shower before making love. Shower together! There's room in there for both of you. Brush your teeth. Use toothpaste and a mouthwash that your spouse approves. Husband, shave within a couple of hours before you have sex! (Unless your wife enjoys the stimulation of making love to a porcupine.) Use deodorant, cologne, and perfume that your spouse really likes. Experiment and find scents that turn each of you on.

Solution #2: Getaway Sex Is Great Sex

Solomon and Shulamith love to get away from the palace and have sex on the road. They know that making love away from home keeps a physical relationship fresh, creative, and exciting.

Solomon (4:8)
"Come with me from Lebanon, my bride,
May you come with me from Lebanon.
Journey down from the summit of Amana,
From the summit of Senir and Hermon,
From the dens of lions,
From the mountains of leopards."

Right in the middle of foreplay in their bedroom in the palace, Solomon invites Shulamith to come with him to the mountains of Lebanon. He wants to take her there and make love to her.

Read this provocative proposal from Shulamith:

Shulamith (7:11–12)

"Come, my beloved, let us go out into the country,

Let us spend the night in the villages.

Let us rise early and go to the vineyards;

Let us see whether the vine has budded

And its blossoms have opened,

And whether the pomegranates have bloomed.

There I will give you my love."

Shulamith asks Solomon to go with her to the country-side and make love outside! Whew! Now, that's true getaway sex!

Schedule at least two getaway weekends a year. More, if you can pull it off. The beach. The mountains. A log cabin. A quaint bed-and-breakfast in an interesting city. Have the grandparents watch the kids, or find a couple you know well and trust, and leave the kids with them. You can return the favor and stay with their kids when they have their getaway.

The sex you have in another place will be invigorating. And, of course, absolutely private. With no kids to worry about, you can spend all the time you want in lovemaking. Maybe even more than once a day. It'll be like the honeymoon all over again. Better, actually, because now you have a clue as to how to please one another in bed.

It can also be a lot of fun to make love in other rooms in your home. Send the kids out on sleepovers, or exploit an opportunity when the kids are involved somewhere, and see what sex is like somewhere else in the house.

Solution #3: Speak Up

In chapters four and seven of the Song, we are given a clear picture of Solomon and Shulamith's foreplay and intercourse. It's surprising how much talking the lovers do during sex.

4:1–7	Solomon praises Shulamith's physical and emotional beauty. He compliments the lovely parts of her body and her character. He starts at her head and slowly moves down her body. His tender and heartfelt praise has three results: it builds her confidence in her beauty; it confirms that he loves all of her and not just her body; and it arouses both of them.
4:9	He tells her how much she arouses him.
4:10–11	He praises her lovemaking and her sensual kisses.
4:13–14	He describes her lovely body and how he's intoxicated by it.
4:15	He acknowledges that she is sexually aroused.
4:16	She speaks, and indicates she's ready for intercourse.

In chapter seven, there is a lot of talking too, and it follows a similar pattern.

7:1–7	Solomon again begins foreplay with praise of Shulamith's physical beauty and her excellent character. This time, he starts at her feet and moves slowly up her body.
7:8–9a	He touches and kisses her breasts and enthusiastically describes their erotic, deep kisses.
7:9b	After intercourse, Shulamith lovingly describes their final kisses as they fall asleep in each other's arms.

Solomon and Shulamith are teaching us not to be afraid to talk during sex. We need to follow their example and talk to express love, to get aroused, to tell each other how we want to be touched, to signal readiness for intercourse, and to reflect on the experience.

Solution #4: Take Your Time in Foreplay

Solomon and Shulamith take their time in foreplay. They are in no hurry. There is no sense of urgency to get to intercourse. In fact, just the opposite. In the two main accounts of their lovemaking (4:1–5:1 and 7:1–9), Solomon and Shulamith go through a progression of steps on their way to intercourse.

First, Solomon verbally praises Shulamith's beauty and her character as he slowly kisses, caresses, and massages the parts of her beautiful body. In 4:1–5, he follows this path down her body: her eyes, hair, teeth, lips, mouth, temples, neck, and breasts. In 7:1–5, he travels the opposite way: her feet, hips, navel, belly, breasts, neck, eyes, nose, head, and hair. There is a slow buildup here of emotional and physical arousal.

Second, Solomon restates his appreciation of Shulamith's beauty.

Solomon (4:7)
"You are altogether beautiful, my darling,
And there is no blemish in you."

(7:6)
"How beautiful and how delightful you are,
My love, with all your charms!"

223

He tells her she is beautiful, both physically and as a person. This is what every wife longs to hear from her husband. And your wife needs to hear it every time you make love.

Third, Solomon continues to praise her body as their physical activity becomes much more intense.

Solomon (4:11a)
"Your lips, my bride, drip honey;
Honey and milk are under your tongue . . ."

(7:8)
"I said, 'I will climb the palm tree,
I will take hold of its fruit stalks.'
Oh, may your breasts be like clusters of the vine . . ."

Fourth, Shulamith becomes sexually aroused.

Solomon (4:15)
"You are a garden spring,
A well of fresh water,
And streams flowing from Lebanon."

Shulamith (4:16)
"Awake, O north wind,
And come, wind of the south;
Make my garden breathe out fragrance,
Let its spices be wafted abroad.
May my beloved come into his garden
And eat its choice fruits!"

Solomon has patiently and lovingly brought her to a state of high physical arousal. Finally, in 5:1, intercourse takes place.

As you see, foreplay is a slow, gentle process. Emotional arousal happens right along with the physical arousal. In the process, you're not only making a physical connection. That can be done quickly. You are making an emotional connection too. Foreplay continues until you both are emotionally and physically ready for intercourse.

All these steps take time.

Solomon (4:6)
> "Until the cool of the day
> When the shadows flee away,
> I will go my way to the mountain of myrrh
> And to the hill of frankincense."

This guy wants to make love to his wife all night long! Great lovemaking requires time. And, boy, does taking time pay off! It does for Solomon and Shulamith. It will for you and your lover too.

Solution #5: Let Yourself Go

Shulamith loves having sex with Solomon. She doesn't do it as a service to him. She loves him and wants to please him, but she also is having a wonderful time in bed with him.

Shulamith is French kissing Solomon (4:11), she is very stimulated and sexually aroused (4:15), she eagerly asks Solomon to come inside her (4:16), and she is completely satisfied and fulfilled with their sex (7:9). She's so happy with her sexual relationship with Solomon that she asks for more (7:10–13).

The question is, wife, how can you feel and respond the way Shulamith does? The answer comes in two parts. First, you and your husband need to carry out Solutions 1–4.

These steps will certainly help. Second, you need to follow Shulamith's example. There are three actions Shulamith does during lovemaking that can help you let yourself go in the bedroom.

The first action is to wear a clean and inviting garment. This kind of outfit will arouse your husband and make you feel sexy.

Solomon (4:11b)

"And the fragrance of your garment is like the fragrance of Lebanon."

Here, Shulamith is wearing a perfumed gown. And Solomon obviously likes it. It sends him through the roof, sexually speaking. We know it's a see-through negligee because, even though she's wearing it (4:1–5), Solomon is able to give a detailed description of her body.

Stop wearing your old poofy, flannel nightgowns during sex. Stop wearing baggy old clothes. Break out your sexy nightgowns. They're way back in the closet. Better yet, buy some new ones. Get your husband's input. He's the expert in this area. What you wear is important.

The second action is to get naked. In 4:12 through 5:1, Shulamith's negligee is removed and she is naked. She is naked throughout the lovemaking account in 7:1–9.

A huge percentage of wives are self-conscious about their bodies and begin to cover up during times of physical intimacy with their husbands. I know, because I've talked to many of them in my office. Here's what I tell them.

"Your husband thinks you're beautiful. Being a male, he's visual and needs to see your body to get sufficiently aroused. Being naked is the ultimate expression of closeness and vulnerability and trust. When you keep clothes on, you are holding back a part of yourself from your husband. You are robbing him and yourself of a full and intimate lovemaking experience. Talk to your husband about it."

The third action is massage. If you haven't tried massage, give it a shot. Massage can progressively relax and stimulate a woman. Break out all those lotions you never use, and ask your husband to give you a ten- to fifteen-minute foreplay massage. He'll love being your personal masseur, and it will help you let go and get fully engaged in sex.

Solution #6: Make It Three in the Bedroom

As we've seen in chapter twelve, God is with the lovers during sex (5:1), and he is the source of their passion (8:6). Based on these biblical truths, I recommend you do one brief and simple action just prior to times of sexual intimacy: hold hands and pray that God will be with you and bless your love-making. Sound crazy? It's not. God, who created the universe, including you both *and* sex, wants to be invited into every aspect of your marriage. He will answer your prayer, and your sex life will receive his supernatural blessing as in all areas of your lives when it is asked. What more could you ask?

Solution #7: Linger and Love

Solomon and Shulamith show us what to do during fore-play and intercourse. They also show us what to do after intercourse.

In 5:1, Solomon stays with Shulamith and talks about their sexual experience:

"I have come into my garden, my sister, my bride;
I have gathered my myrrh along with my balsam.

I have eaten my honeycomb and my honey;
I have drunk my wine and my milk."

Again, after they've had intercourse, the two lovers stay together and do some more loving:

Shulamith (7:9b)
"It goes down smoothly, for my beloved,
Flowing gently through the lips of those who fall asleep."

She is describing their final, gentle kisses as they drop off to sleep in each other's arms.

The lesson? After intercourse, stay with each other and bask in the afterglow. Talk about how great your physical intimacy was. Hold each other. Do some more kissing and caressing. This will enhance your lovemaking and prepare you for the next time.

21

Don't Quit, and *Do* What the Song Says

The world is full of quitters. As a clinical psychologist specializing in marriage therapy, I see my share of quitters. They fall into two groups.

The first group is made up of those spouses who want to quit and get divorced. They come to my office to tell me why divorce is their only option. Here are some of the most common reasons these quitters use to end a marriage:

"I don't love you anymore."*

"We've grown apart."

*I wrote a book I titled *I Don't Love You Anymore* for those who need to know what to do when they are told these words by their spouses.

"I never loved you."

"I felt pressured to marry you."

"We are two different persons."

"Persons just can't change."

"I feel trapped."

"I need space."

"I need to find myself."

"It's not you; it's me."

"I'm just not good for you."

"You're not intellectually stimulating."

"I've grown beyond you."

"I'm having a midlife crisis."

"I love you like a brother (or sister)."

"I love you as the parent of our children."

"I love you, but I'm not in love with you."

"I don't love you the way a spouse should love you."

"I think God wants me to be happy."

"It's better for the kids, because our bad marriage is hurting them."

These "reasons" are nothing more than ridiculous, petty, and selfish rationalizations for a sinful choice. These quitters state their marriage-ending case and fully expect me to agree with them. They are disappointed.

My response is always the same: "Is that all you have? Can't you do any better? You don't have to get a divorce. With God's help and the right steps, you can build a great marriage. The best marriage any couple ever had."

The spouses who want to quit and yet stay married is the second group of quitters. They choose to settle for a middle of the road, mediocre, or even miserable marriage. Here are the top four reasons I've heard from this second group of quitters:

"We're staying together for the kids."

"We can't afford to get divorced."

"We'll stay married, because it is the right thing to do."

"This is the best marriage we can hope to have and it will have to do."

I'm sure Sandy would be thrilled to know that I'm staying with her because of the kids. Or, because of money. Or, because it's the right thing to do. Or, because our marriage is as good as it's going to get, and we just have to accept it. She'd be hurt and insulted beyond belief by these pitiful statements. And she ought to be. These so-called reasons have nothing to do with a real love relationship.

I say virtually the same thing to these quitters as I do to the first group of quitters: "You don't have to settle for this type of pathetic marriage. With God's help and the right steps, you can build a great marriage. The best marriage any couple ever had."

There's a very simple reason why I can tell spouses that God wants them to have a great marriage. It's because I'm not saying it. It's God. He delivered this message three thousand years ago in the Song of Solomon. And he hasn't changed his mind. Here are God's words, communicated through Shulamith:

Shulamith (8:6–7)

"Put me like a seal over your heart,

Like a seal on your arm.

For love is as strong as death . . .

Its flashes are flashes of fire,
The very flame of the Lord.
Many waters cannot quench love,
Nor will rivers overflow it;
If a man were to give all the riches of his house for
love,
It would be utterly despised."

What a marvelous definition of the nature of real love! Solomon and Shulamith have it all! They enjoy an intense, powerful love fueled by God himself. It's the kind of love we all desperately want and need. And it's the kind of love God desires all of us to experience. Two words jump out at me in these two verses.

Permanence

The first word is *permanence*. Love is like an unbreakable seal bonding two hearts together. Love, like death, is final and cannot be reversed. You can dump oceans and oceans of water on love, and it will never be extinguished.

God is not interested only in permanence, however. Many couples stay married for a lifetime, but their marriages are lousy. Marriage is not about earning a longevity pin.

Passion

The second word completes God's definition of marital love. That word is *passion*. Real love in marriage is a burning flame of passion, kept alive by God and his instructions for maintaining that love for a lifetime. Passion is what makes a marriage great!

The Wonderful News

The wonderful news is that Song of Solomon 8:6–7 doesn't have to describe just Solomon and Shulamith's love. It can also describe you and your spouse's love.

God's message through the Song is that a permanent and passionate love is available to *every married couple* willing to follow the example he gave us in Solomon and Shulamith.

You know how to create an incredible love. Now, there is only one question. Will you do what the Song says?

Appendix A

Beginning a Relationship with God

Here are the simple facts concerning how to establish a relationship with God through his Son, Jesus.

You are a sinner. So am I. So is everyone. You've made mistakes and done things wrong in your life, haven't you? Well, even one mistake, one sin, separates you from God. On your own, there is no way to reach a holy and perfect God. Romans 3:23 drives this point home: "For all have sinned and fall short of the glory of God."

God could have left you in your sin, condemned never to know him, and to die and go to hell forever. But he didn't do that. God loves you so much that he sent his only Son, Jesus, to earth, to die for your sins. Because Jesus paid the penalty for your sins, you don't have to be eternally separated from

God. "For the wages of sin is death. But the free gift of God is eternal life in Christ Jesus our Lord" (Rom. 6:23).

First Corinthians 15:3–4 spells out the truth that we must believe in order to know God and enter his family: "Christ died for our sins according to the Scriptures, and . . . He was buried and . . . He was raised on the third day."

Do you want all your sins, the ones you've already committed and the ones you will commit for the rest of your life, wiped away? Do you want the God-given ability to resist sin? Do you want to know God personally? Do you want God's power to energize your life here on earth? If you answered yes to these questions, then you're ready to come to Christ.

Let me suggest a prayer for you to begin a relationship with God. (It's not the words that will save you. It is what you are choosing in your heart and your mind.)

God,

I'm a sinner. I've made mistakes and sinned. I know that my sin separates me from you. I can't reach you on my own. Thank you for sending Jesus as the only way for me to get to know you. I believe that Jesus died on the cross for my sins, and I accept him as my Savior. I believe that Jesus rose from the dead, proving he is God and has the power to forgive my sins. I'm tired of living my life my way. I now give my life to you, God.

Amen.

Other Books by Dr. David Clarke

Men are Clams, Women are Crowbars
    A study guide for couples and groups is also available
A Marriage After God's Own Heart
    Follow-up materials for couples and groups are also
    available
I Don't Love You Anymore
Parenting Isn't for Super Heroes
The Total Marriage Makeover
The Six Steps to Emotional Freedom
Cinderella Meets the Caveman

To schedule a seminar, order Dr. Clarke's books, or download audio of his talks, please contact:

David Clarke Seminars
www.davidclarkeseminars.com
1-888-516-8844

or

Marriage & Family Enrichment Center
6505 North Himes Ave.
Tampa, FL 33614

Dr. David Clarke is a Christian psychologist, speaker, and the author of seven books, including *Men Are Clams, Women Are Crowbars*, *A Marriage after God's Own Heart*, and *Winning the Parenting War*. A graduate of Dallas Theological Seminary and Western Conservative Baptist Seminary, he has been in full-time private practice for over twenty years. Through his entertaining and practical seminars, he presents God's truth in the areas of emotional well being, relationship building, and the development of parenting skills. He lives in Tampa, Florida, with his family.